Michael DeFazio

Jesus in 3D
© 2011 by Michael DeFazio. All rights reserved.

Published by Real Life Church
23841 Newhall Ranch Road
Valencia, CA 91355
www.reallifechurch.org

Published in association with Samizdat Creative
5441 South Knox Court
Littleton, CO 49203
www.samizdatcreative.com

ISBN-13: 9780983328032

Cover design by Joshua Heyer
www.heyerdesign.com

To Beth and Claire

I hope this is only one of many ways
I help you see Jesus more clearly.

Contents

Introduction

About a year ago I saw my first 3D movie. (Yes, I know, I'm a little behind.) The film was beautiful, but after a while I got a bit tired of it. So I took off my 3D glasses to see if I could enjoy the film without them. I could see the basic images and for the most part follow the movement, but focusing was very difficult and I about gave myself a headache. So I gave up, put the glasses back on, and took in the rest of the show.

Reading the Gospel stories of Jesus is for many of you not unlike watching a 3D movie without wearing 3D glasses. You can make out a few details and get a vague sense of what's going on, but the whole screen is fairly distorted and if you stare too long, your head starts to hurt.

I hope this book changes that. Its purpose is to take a close look at Jesus as a real person—the real person you read about in Matthew, Mark, Luke, and John.[1] These four books tell the story of Jesus, and this story inspires, encourages, enlightens, and even transforms us. But it also confuses us.

I (perhaps naïvely) believe anyone will benefit from reading this book, but I'm especially writing to you who have read the Gospels and walked away confused. Maybe you love a verse or two from Matthew or Mark, or perhaps a story from Luke or John. But even the parts you love feel like individual puzzle pieces without a box top to clarify how they fit together.

---

[1] I believe Jesus was more than just a man. I believe, in fact, that he was and is the incarnation of the one true God and the exact representation of God's being. But he also was and is a real person. He lived, ate, and slept. He laughed, drank, and wept. He did some pretty impressive stuff and led a revolution of sorts, but wound up getting himself killed. Then God raised him from the dead. But through it all—from the beginning of his life on down to the present—he remained 100% human. Without denying the divinity of Jesus, this book focuses on his humanity.

The box top you're looking for is something Jesus called the "kingdom of God." Or to return to our original metaphor, if Jesus' mission is a 3D film, God's kingdom is a pair of 3D glasses. It integrates the individual layers of color to form a single coherent image.

Some of you have never thought twice about the kingdom of God, even if you've gone to church your whole life. This is kind of weird, considering that the kingdom of God formed the centerpiece of Jesus' entire movement. If you don't believe me, check out the following list of some of the many ways we see Jesus and the Gospel writers talking about God's kingdom.

(1) How Jesus began his ministry: *"The time has come. The **kingdom of God** has come near. Repent and believe the good news!"* (Mark 1.14-15; also Matthew 4.17[2])

(2) What God sent Jesus to do: *"I must proclaim the good news of the **kingdom of God** to the other towns also, because that is why I was sent."* (Luke 4.43)

(3) What Jesus actually did: *Jesus traveled about from one town and village to another, proclaiming the good news of **the kingdom of God**.* (Luke 8.1)

(4) What Jesus said to seek above all else: *"But seek first **his kingdom** and his righteousness, and all these things will be given to you as well."* (Matthew 6.33)

(5) What Jesus sent his disciples to proclaim: *When Jesus had called the Twelve together . . . he sent them out to proclaim the **kingdom of God** and to heal the sick.* (Luke 9.1-2, 61; also Matthew 10.5-8)

(6) The center of Jesus' model prayer: *"Our Father in heaven, hallowed be your name, **your kingdom** come, your will be done, on earth as it is in heaven."* (Matthew 6.9-10)

---

[2] Matthew often uses the phrase "kingdom of heaven" instead of "kingdom of God." There is no difference between the two. Matthew replaces "God" with "heaven" out of reverence for God's name. The Jewish people had a history of not saying God's name because of its sacredness, and Matthew's readers were mostly Jewish. Also, anytime you see a portion of Scripture highlighted, the emphasis is my own.

(7) The meaning of Jesus' miracles and exorcisms: *"But if I drive out demons by the finger of God, then the **kingdom of God** has come upon you."* (Luke 11.20; Matthew 12.28)

(8) The subject of Jesus' parables: *"The knowledge of the secrets of the **kingdom of God** has been given to you, but to others I speak in parables."* (Luke 8.9; also Matthew 13)

(9) How Jesus explains his defenseless acceptance of death: *"**My kingdom** is not of this world. If it were, my servants would fight to prevent my arrest by the Jewish leaders. But now **my kingdom** is from another place."* (John 18.36)

(10) The summary of Jesus' ministry: *Jesus went throughout Galilee, teaching in their synagogues, proclaiming the good news of **the kingdom**, and healing every disease and sickness among the people.* (Matthew 4.23; 9.35)

Clearly, God's kingdom was a big deal to Jesus. But what is it?

Jesus never defines it, no doubt in part because a definition alone could never tell the whole story. It might help us get a good start though, so I'm going to give it a shot. Building especially on Jesus' model prayer, here is our working definition of the kingdom of God: *the realm over which God rules as king, where his name is properly honored and his will is promptly done.* — definition of KOG

I'll spend the rest of this book unpacking what that means. In chapter one, I'll overview the story of God up to the coming of Jesus. (In other words, the whole Old Testament in about twenty pages!) Chapter two will explore the first century world of Jesus — what expectations they had for someone like him. The next three chapters lay out four interlocking goals of Jesus' mission: establish God's kingdom and reform God's family (three), warn of God's judgment (four), and clarify God's will (five). The final two chapters examine the meaning of Jesus' death (six) and the impact of his resurrection (seven). By the end, you'll have a better grasp not only of the individual elements of Jesus' agenda, but also how they fit together within the overall story of God's search for a kingdom.

One

WHAT STORY DOES JESUS FULFILL?

Talking about Jesus today is both difficult and easy. Easy because everyone seems to love Jesus. Difficult because the Jesus most people love bears a shadowy resemblance to the real thing. Search for "Jesus" online and in one-tenth of a second you'll discover nearly 200,000 options to explore. The images alone will make your head spin in confusion (or shake in disgust), and not just because of the amount of Jesuses but the variety as well. You'll see laughing Jesus, crying Jesus, serious Jesus, smiling Jesus, black Jesus, white Jesus, warrior Jesus, hippie Jesus, biker Jesus, business Jesus, Native American Jesus, Middle Eastern Jesus, iconic Jesus, cartoon Jesus, even — and perhaps most tellingly — Play-Doh Jesus.

There seem to be as many profiles of Jesus as there are people talking about him. What's worse, the underlying question has become, "What kind of Jesus do you *want*?" Folks have always disagreed about different aspects of Jesus' identity and work, but today much of the Jesus conversation has been hi-jacked by "consumerism." This is just a fancy way of saying that most of us construct an image of Jesus that matches what we already desire. Do you want soul-saving Jesus or world-changing Jesus, Jesus who rides a donkey or one who prefers an elephant, a Mr. Universe double or a Gandhi look-alike? All this begs the question of how to navigate our path through the many faces of Jesus and discern the truth of who he was and is.

Things don't get much easier when it comes to Jesus' message about God's kingdom. While virtually all scholars agree that proclaiming and manifesting God's kingdom was central to Jesus' ministry, beyond this small consensus we find many disputes. Is the kingdom of God heavenly or earthly? Present or future? Political or spiritual? Personal or communal? Or more to the point, in what ways is it a combination of all these things (and many more besides)?

Remember our working definition of God's kingdom: *the realm over which God rules as king, where his name is properly honored and his will is promptly done.* Given that God created the universe to be his kingdom (as we'll soon discover), in one sense the "kingdom of God" is a way of talking about the world as he intended it to be. But keeping the matter this general isn't enough. We must be more rooted and specific if we want to understand what Jesus came here to do.

MORE TO THE STORY?

Remembering a simple fact of communication may help us: Most statements can't be properly understood apart from the context or story in which they find a home. Much of the time we recognize this instinctively. For instance, the words "I have a dream" by themselves could mean anything. But in the context of a certain Alabama preacher's struggle for racial equality in 20th century America, they take on very specific content. They find a home here, and here they say something they don't say anywhere else.

Similarly, if I told you that Frodo and Sam reached Mount Doom and successfully destroyed the One Ring created to rule them all, you'd need to know the *Lord of the Rings* story to make heads or tails of my declaration. There are endless examples— "We're not in Kansas anymore," "I'm gonna make him an offer he can't refuse," red pill or blue pill?—but you get the point. Statements don't make sense apart from the context or story in which they belong.

This matters in our search for the real Jesus because when he arrived on the scene announcing, *"The time has come. The kingdom of God has come near. Repent and believe the good news!"* (Mark 1.14-

15), his words hardly came from nowhere. His announcement of the arrival of God's kingdom marks a climactic moment in a certain story, and without this story we risk missing Jesus.

CLUES FROM THE GOSPELS

If you were going to tell someone the story of Jesus, where would you begin? What would you say first? How would you open your presentation or start the conversation? The authors of our Gospels clearly wrestled with these questions. All four of them open differently, each one making unique and complementary points in line with their distinct portraits of Jesus. Yet in their own unique ways, each of the Gospels begins by drawing attention to a simple but substantial fact: The Jesus story belongs within a much larger story of what God had been doing for quite some time.

Matthew wastes no time in framing his Jesus story within the history of Abraham and his descendants. The second word of Matthew's Gospel is "genealogy" or *geneseos*, which comes from the Greek word *genesis*. Sound familiar? Matthew then ties Jesus to two central figures from biblical history, both of whom figure prominently in his upcoming family tree: *Jesus the Messiah, the son of David, the son of Abraham* (Mt 1.1). Matthew rounds out this opening section with a well-crafted list of characters from Israel's history—some more memorable (and easier to pronounce!) than others—and these many stories together tell the one story of God's relationship with his people.[1]

Unlike Matthew, Mark is in too much of a hurry to bother with a long list of names. Instead he immediately points out how the very beginnings of Jesus' story must be understood in relation to ancient promises given by God through Israel's

---

[1] Throughout this book I'll talk a lot about Israel, Israelites, the Jews, God's people, etc. So let me clarify a few things up front. I am not talking about the modern state of Israel or its citizens. When I talk about "Israel" or "Israelites" or "Jews," I am referring to the people of God in the Old Testament. Once Jesus came and fulfilled God's calling on Israel, God's family opened up to both Jews and Gentiles (the rest of us). Our identity in God's family is about Jesus, not ethnicity. I also at times use "Israel" to refer to the geographical region in which many of the Bible's events took place.

prophets. Notice his first words: *The beginning of the good news about Jesus the Messiah,* **as it is written in Isaiah the prophet.** Apparently some knowledge of this Israelite prophet named Isaiah — and in turn the world in which he prophesied — will help us know this Messiah named Jesus.

Luke's opening scenes provide many clues like this, but let's stick to one hint we find in the first line of his work: *Many have undertaken to draw up an account of the things that have been fulfilled among us.* For our purposes the key word here is *fulfilled.* You only talk about things having been fulfilled in the present in relation to promises made in the past. In other words, once again you must know the story into which Jesus born and the promises made there in order to understand who he is.

For John's part, we don't even need the entire opening sentence. The first three words will do: *In the beginning.* The rest of John's opening poem (1.1-18) overflows with allusions to the sacred history of God, from the moment of creation on down.

In these different ways, Matthew, Mark, Luke, and John impress upon us that understanding Jesus requires paying close attention to the unfolding history of God's relationship with the world, and specifically his people Israel. This story has been preserved for us in the Old Testament, and right now we're going to take a bird's eye view of the whole thing. If you've ever wondered how in the world it all fits together, this next section is for you!

THE STORY OF GOD

Remember, we're trying to find the right home for Jesus' declaration, *"The time has come. The kingdom of God has come near. Repent and believe the good news"* (Mark 1.14-15). Something *has come near* that wasn't previously here, and that "something" is the realm over which God rules, where his name is rightly honored and his will is promptly done. Following leads from Matthew, Mark, Luke, and John, we're fleshing this out by exploring the story of God as told in the Scriptures. For the sake of clarity, let's break this story down into three acts.

ACT I:
GOD CREATED THE HEAVENS AND THE EARTH

CREATION

This story begins, well, at the beginning. *In the beginning God created the heavens and the earth* (Genesis 1.1). The inaugural scene of this story is the opening scene of history. And the way the Bible depicts this scene emphasizes one fact in particular — that God alone is king of all creation. God is the universe's monarch, chief, sovereign, or lord. The Bible's first chapter has been masterfully composed to convey the kingship of God.

Take a look at Genesis 1, and notice first how this story has only one God. This may seem obvious and not worthy of much *Monotheistic* attention. But in its original context the one-of-a-kind God-ness of God would immediately stand out as the strangest feature of a creation story. Most folks in the ancient world told epic tales of the world's beginning, and their stories all shared certain features. One of these features was the multiplicity of the gods.

One ancient version called *Enuma Elish* begins with a genealogy of various gods and goddesses. From there the story gets complicated (almost like a soap opera, as you'll soon see!) so bear with me for a minute. The two oldest deities were Apsu and Tiamat, each of whom supervised different bodies of water. The mingling of their waters produced lots of offspring — other gods and goddesses. Apsu (the dad) eventually got tired of hearing all the kids' noise and so he plotted to kill them. His wife objected, but he continued with his plans. As we would expect, Tiamat wasn't going to stand by and let this happen! She consulted Ea, a god of wisdom, who responded by reciting a magic spell that killed Apsu.

The problem with this was that Tiamat didn't want Apsu *dead*, she just didn't want him killing their kids. So Tiamat, who was more powerful than Apsu, decided to go after Ea. Ea was in trouble until a "hero" named Marduk (one of Ea's children) stepped up in his defense. Marduk struck a deal with all of them that if he proved victorious, he would be considered *king of all the gods*. I'll spare you the gory details of the battle between Marduk's and Tiamat's forces, but the short version is that Marduk won.

After Marduk defeated Tiamat, he split her body in half. From one half he fashioned the heavens, and from the other he formed the earth. Then from the blood Tiamat's military general Marduk made humans to serve the gods so they could rest.[2]

Seems pretty strange, right? It was perfectly normal to ancient folks though. And since *this* was their normal, *our* story seems odd. No competition between gods. No martial victory establishing one god's dominance over the others. No carnage preceding the formation of heaven and earth.

On the contrary, in our story there is only one God, and this one God creates everything that exists. As such, he is by definition *king of all things.*

The second detail that draws attention to the kingship of God concerns the way God speaks. When God speaks, stuff happens.[3] When God says, "Let there be light or vegetation," light or vegetation immediately appears. This, too, lines up perfectly with ancient notions of kingship. When the king speaks, his words are immediately obeyed.

In the movie *A Knight's Tale,* a poor thatcher's son named William falsely portrays himself as a knight—Ulrich von Liechtenstein—in order to joust in tournaments for "riches and glory." But eventually William's deceit comes to light and he is placed in stocks to await execution. As the crowd mocks him only days after singing his praises, a disguised man reveals himself as the royal Edward, Black Prince of Wales. Edward steps forward and claims that his own records show that William's ancestry stretches back to an "ancient royal line" that restores his status as a knight. It doesn't matter that everyone knows such a bloodline didn't exist, for as Prince Edward declares, "This is my word, and as such it is beyond contestation."

God speaks. And what God says happens, because God is king.

---

[2] You can read about all this and more in a very helpful little book called *How to Read Genesis* by Tremper Longman III (Downers Grove: IVP, 2005).

[3] Another important feature is that God refers to himself as "us." God will reveal that he is and has always been what we call the "Trinity," which means there is both a threeness (Father, Son, Holy Spirit) and a oneness to his identity. Many have read this later theology back onto Genesis 1, and this kind of reading certainly has its place. But original hearers would recognize in this "us" the normal way kings speak. Sometimes this "us" referred to the king acting in concert with his royal court. Other times it would simply be a poetic way of referring to his superior power and authority. In this way, too, God is talking like the good king that he is.

Third, Genesis 1 shows God making heaven and earth much (3)
like a king would construct a temple. In the ancient world kings
and temples always went hand in hand (like in Psalm 48). In the
case of this original building project, note especially the way days
one through three parallel days four through six. It's as if God
framed his temple in the first half of the week, and then filled it
during the second half. Look at the two panels below and notice
how day four corresponds to day one, day five to day two, and
day six to day three. God was artfully constructing an earthly
dwelling for his heavenly presence.

FRAMING	FILLING
Day 1 (1.3-5) light/darkness	**Day 4** (1.14-19) sun/moon/stars
Day 2 (1.6-8) water/sky	**Day 5** (1.20-23) fish/birds
Day 3 (1.9-13) dry ground / vegetation	**Day 6** (1.24-31) land animals / humanity

The prophet Isaiah once spoke on God's behalf to some folks who
wanted to build him an earthly temple: *This is what the LORD says:
"Heaven is my throne, and the earth is my footstool. Where is the house
you will build for me? Where will my resting place be? Has not my
hand made all these things, and so they came into being?" declares the
LORD* (Isaiah 66.1-2). In other words, don't worry about building
me a tiny little temple on earth because I've already built one for
myself — heaven and earth as a whole!

The fourth element of Act One that reveals the kingship of (4)
God has to do with you and me. Together, as male and female,
we were created *in God's image*. Take a look at Genesis 1.26-27:

*Then God said, "Let us make human beings in our image, in
our likeness, so that they may rule over the fish in the sea and
the birds in the sky, over the livestock and all the wild animals,
and over all the creatures that move along the ground."*

So God created human beings in his own image,
in the image of God he created them;
male and female he created them.

In the ancient world, the only person "created in God's image" was the king. His job was to embody the reign of God — or the gods — in this world. He was their royal representative. Most people believed that his earthly rule manifested their heavenly rule. This explains why he was so revered!

Interestingly enough the Bible takes the idea of divinely-appointed kingship and applies it to the entire human family. Not just one of us, but everyone together has been given the royal task of ruling on God's behalf. Notice how God created humanity *so that they may* **rule** . . . *God blessed them and said to them, "Be fruitful and increase in number; fill the earth and subdue it.* **Rule over the fish in the sea and the birds in the sky and over every living creature that moves on the ground"** (Genesis 1.26, 28). Being created in God's image means representing God's loving reign to each other and to the created world — including mountains, oceans, roses, daisies, cornfields, pasta, cows, pigs, lizards, and dogs. (We could go on, but you get the point!). We have been appointed to carry out this task. This mission has been entrusted to us all.

Once again we must be clear about the overall point Genesis is making. In all the ways we just noted, God's creation of heaven and earth reveal God alone as the world's rightful king. One of Israel's poets later puts this thought to music: *For the LORD is the great God, the great King above all gods. In his hand are the depths of the earth, and the mountain peaks belong to him. The sea is his, for he made it, and his hands formed the dry land* (Psalm 95.3-5). Heaven and earth together are God's kingdom — the realm over which God rules as king, where his name is properly honored and his will is promptly done. This, however, is only the beginning of the story, which soon takes a tragic twist.

ACT II:
FALL  HUMANS REBELLED AND CORRUPTED GOD'S GOOD WORLD

The final word spoken over God's completed creation was not simply *good* but *very good* (Gen 1.28). In Genesis 2, we find God's royal representatives getting along quite nicely: naming the animals, finding and enjoying one another, producing offspring, and so forth. But the final word of that first week turns out to be the first word of the world's long history. The goodness doesn't last. By the time we get to Genesis 6, God's evaluation couldn't be more different:

> The LORD saw how great the wickedness of the human race had become on the earth, and that every inclination of the thoughts of the human heart was only evil all the time. The LORD regretted that he had made human beings on the earth, and his heart was deeply troubled.... Now the earth was corrupt in God's sight and was full of violence. God saw how corrupt the earth had become, for all the people on earth had corrupted their ways. (Genesis 6.5-6, 11-12)

How did we get from *very good* in Genesis 1 to *corrupt and full of violence* in Genesis 6? This "fall" began, of course, with Adam and Eve—God's original junior partners in his creation-as-kingdom adventure. God planted Adam and Eve in the Garden of Eden with only one limitation. They were not to eat from one tree in the garden's center: *the tree of the knowledge of good and evil.* If they did, they would die. Some time after God made known his commands, a serpent—the craftiest animal of all—subtly planted seeds of doubt in Eve's mind about God's motive and truthfulness. The serpent said that when she ate this tree's fruit she would not die but *become like God* knowing both good and evil. The temptation was too much for her, she ate, and Adam followed suit. Immediately they sensed their nakedness and hid. God discovered their disobedience, listened as they blamed each other and then the serpent, and then verbalized the curse their actions brought upon all creation. The folks God formed to help establish his kingdom decided instead to go their own way, and the world has been recovering ever since.

If we know ourselves well, we certainly recognize our own story in theirs. It begins with a whisper, a serpentine voice subtly suggesting that God may not be as good and trustworthy as we'd hoped. Maybe he's holding out on us. Maybe his rules are arbitrary, designed as mechanisms of social control to keep us childishly dependent on him. Maybe he doesn't have our best interests in mind, but only his own. For any number of reasons—all traceable to our fear-inspired desire for independence from God or anything else that might limit us—we listen to that voice. We act in concert with the Enemy's enticement, only to later find ourselves broken, damaged, and exposed. Yes, the story of Adam and Eve is also the story of you and me.

The rest of Genesis 3-11 traces the downward spiral of sin's poisoning effect. It portrays in narrative form the ongoing corruption of God's good world. Everything you'd expect to see is here: jealousy, murder, deceit, revenge, disrespect, anger, and arrogance. Creation's relational harmony has been thoroughly disrupted at every turn: God to humankind, humans to each other, each of us to ourselves, and all of us to the created world we call home. What was supposed to be God's kingdom has become instead a monument to our foolish and ultimately destructive grasps for life and power of our own making.

ACT III:
GOD CHOSE TO RESCUE THE WORLD THROUGH ISRAEL

As we continue our walk through the Old Testament, let's pause to remember what we're doing. Our goal is to gain a clearer picture of Jesus. We don't just want a Jesus that fits our preferences and desires. We want the truth. And we realize that discerning which Jesus is true begins by asking what story he came to fulfill. So far we've found that the story starts with God's creation of everything, and in particular with human beings as the ones commissioned to extend God's kingdom throughout the earth. And we've also seen that, to put it simply, we screwed everything up.

Thankfully, however, the story of God doesn't end with our rebellion and its deteriorating effects. In fact, in many ways the first eleven chapters preface the real story to be told.

Act III, Scene I: God promised to bless the whole world through Abraham's family

The story of God's redemptive interaction with a particular group of people begins in Genesis 12 when God spoke to a man named Abram.

The LORD had said to Abram, "Go from your country, your people and your father's household to the land I will show you.

I will make you into a great nation,
and I will bless you;
I will make your name great,
and you will be a blessing.
I will bless those who bless you,
and whoever curses you I will curse;
and all peoples on earth
will be blessed through you."

God called Abram, whom he later renamed Abraham, and told him to take a walk. Abraham didn't get to know where he was going. All he knew was that as he went, he travelled with the promise that his family would be the vessel through which God would *bless* all the other families on earth. Apparently this was enough for Abraham, because he packed up and walked away from everything he had and knew in simple obedience to God's command.

Everything that happens from this point in Genesis to the end of Revelation reveals the story of what God has done (and is still doing) to overcome the problems of sin and evil and death depicted in Genesis 3-11. In this regard the word *bless* marks a key turning point. Five times in God's call to Abraham we see this word, which corresponds to the five times in Genesis 1-11 we hear of God's *curse*. The curse is profoundly powerful but stronger still is God's blessing, and this blessing demands the last word. God's *blessing* upon Abraham and all his friends also recalls God's original blessing of Adam and Eve in Genesis 1. In Abraham, God began actively turning back the tables on evil, working to overcome sin's effects and restore his world to what he initially intended. Once again God set in motion his original plan to bless humanity as they resumed the purpose for which he created them — the extension of God's kingdom throughout the earth. *↪With the hope of not destroying creation!*

In promising Abraham that through his descendants God's blessing would reach the world, God yoked himself to this particular family. The remainder of Genesis records the unfolding history of God's relationship to Abraham's descendants: Isaac, Jacob, and Jacob's twelve sons who will

[handwritten margin notes: Abraham's blessing is intended to reverse the curse]

23

become the twelve tribes of Israel. It's fascinating (and sometimes scandalous!) reading, but for now let's jump ahead to the end. Genesis closes with God's people in what seems to be a good place—a position of power within the kingdom of Egypt, with Jacob's son Joseph serving at the right hand of the Egyptian King (or "Pharaoh").

However, the opening scene of the Bible's next book confirm what by now we suspect to be a pattern: Good moments don't last forever. Eventually a new king assumed Egypt's throne and he didn't care about the former king's alliance with Joseph. He saw only that these pesky Israelites were growing into a serious threat. So like any normal king, he enslaved them in order to keep them under control. Four hundred years later, God's people have been reduced to brickmakers constructing monuments to Egypt's glory and fame. So the Israelites cried out for relief.

Act III, Scene II: God called Moses and delivered Israel from slavery in Egypt

God *saw* the misery of his people, *heard* their cries of oppression, and *was concerned* about their suffering (Exodus 3.7-8). So he appeared in a burning bush to the fugitive Moses and said, *"The cry of the Israelites has reached me, and I have seen the way the Egyptians are oppressing them. So now, go. I am sending you to Pharaoh to bring my people the Israelites out of Egypt"* (3.9-10). To make a long story short, Moses eventually obeyed, showed up at Pharaoh's palace, and demanded the release of God's people so they could worship God freely. After Pharaoh's initial dismissal, God demonstrated his power in marvelously frightening ways, so Pharaoh agreed to set them free the next day. When morning came, however, he changed his mind. This cycle repeated itself multiple times until Pharaoh eventually relented. Very soon, however, he mourned the loss of his labor force and sent Egypt's troops to recapture Israel. At this point God famously parted the waters of the sea and Israel walked across on dry land. But when the Egyptian soldiers followed, the waters rushed back to their place. Israel was free.

"Exodus" is the name given to the events constituting this liberation (and the biblical book that recounts it), and this exodus becomes the Old Testament story's central event. Everything that comes before — including creation itself — has been told in a way that points forward to this moment; everything that follows recollects it, and either attempts to embody it faithfully or eagerly anticipates its repetition. Let's focus on three features of the original exodus event.

First, central to the Exodus story was a showdown between ① the God of Moses and the gods of Pharaoh. Central to this *Confronting* showdown was a series of plagues God inflicted upon Egypt: the Nile turning to blood, infestations of frogs, gnats, and flies, the *false Gs* death of livestock, boils on their skin, hail, locusts, darkness, and the death of every firstborn son. We read in Exodus 12.12 that through these wonders God was bringing *judgment on all the gods of Egypt*, which in part meant exposing the emptiness of their claims to power.

Also remember that in the ancient world the gods' royal power was believed to rest on earthly kings such as Pharaoh. So it comes as no surprise that God's battle with Egypt's gods involved God in a faceoff with Pharaoh in particular. When Pharaoh first heard God's demand through Moses, he defiantly scoffed, *"Who is the LORD, that I should obey him and let Israel go? I do not know the LORD and I will not let Israel go"* (Exodus 5.2). Yet as the Bible repeatedly and ironically makes plain, God would have Pharaoh and all his people *know* exactly who he was (7.5; 8.10, 22; 9.14, 30; 10.2). Almost to the point of rubbing it in, God revealed that regardless of what Pharaoh may think about his current place in the kingdom, *God* raised him to this position for one reason: *"That I might show you my power and that my name might be proclaimed in all the earth"* (9.16). God would have Pharaoh acknowledge God's sovereignty over his own. And, of course, Pharaoh did.

Second, God provided a way for his people to avoid his ② judgment upon Egypt's gods. When God struck down all the *Protecting* firstborn males, the Israelites were protected by marking their *his* doorframes with the blood of sacrificial lambs. In this way God *people* rescued Israel from his judgment upon Egypt's imperial arrogance and unjust oppression.

Third, this act of deliverance and rescue once again ③ confirmed God's choosing of Israel as his special people for his *Election* special program. He didn't covenant himself with them because *of Israel* of their superior power or intrinsic attractiveness. He did so

25

solely on the basis of unmerited love and faithfulness to his earlier promises. God's overall purposes for creation put his commitment to Israel in proper perspective. God liberated her to continue his mission of forming a people to embody and extend his kingdom throughout the world.

As a matter of fact, God told Israel this before he gave her the Ten Commandments that formed the foundation of their Law (or "Torah"). We find the Ten Commandments in Exodus 20, just a few short chapters after God saved his people out of Egypt. Notice what God says in Exodus 19.3-6, just before revealing these mandates for Israel's life together:

> Then Moses went up to God, and the LORD called to him from the mountain and said, "This is what you are to say to the house of Jacob and what you are to tell the people of Israel: 'You yourselves have seen what I did to Egypt, and how I carried you on eagles' wings and brought you to myself. **Now if you obey me fully and keep my covenant, then out of all nations you will be my treasured possession. Although the whole earth is mine, you will be for me a kingdom of priests and a holy nation.'** These are the words you are to speak to the Israelites."

Israel would be for God _a kingdom of priests_. What does that mean? We've defined what "kingdom" means, and "priests" were called to mediate God's presence to others. So Israel was to become the realm over which God rules, where his name is properly honored and his will is promptly done, and in this way she would mediate God's presence to the world. Once again God hit the reset button and took another step forward in his pursuit of a faithful kingdom.

It was for this task that God gave Israel the Law, meant not as a burden to drive them to despair, but rather as a guide for building their life together in this new kingdom. This Law called them to be holy — different, unique, set apart — because the LORD their God was different from their neighbors' gods (Leviticus 11.44). The Law emphasized forgiveness and reconciliation through an elaborate sacrificial system, justice for the poor through recurring debt cancellations, and sexual holiness in the midst of a world engaged in anti-creational sexual sin. If you've ever tried to read through the Bible's first few books, you know that some of these laws are incredibly strange! But their big-picture purpose was clear. They were supposed to shape Israel into a countercultural community where people could see God.

From here let's pick up a little speed. After wandering through the desert for forty years learning all sorts of valuable (and frustrating) things about themselves and God, the Israelites approached the edge of the land God promised to Abraham. Just then Moses died and Joshua took over and led Israel's conquest of their Promised Land. Once settled, the twelve tribes divvied up the land, each receiving a portion according to size, preference, and need (except for the priestly tribe of the Levites, whose portion was God alone). For a while Israel was governed by leaders called "judges." God worked through these judges to once again (and again, and then again) deliver Israel from the oppressive messes she brought on by persistently disobeying God. After this cycle of sin-judgment-repentance-deliverance recurred at least a dozen times, Israel decided the time has come for a change.

Act III, Scene III: God accepted rejection and allowed Israel to have a king

The change they sought, however, turned out not to be God's favorite idea. Israel asked for a king. Here is how the story unfolds in 1 Samuel 8.1-9:

> When Samuel grew old, he appointed his sons as Israel's leaders. The name of his firstborn was Joel and the name of his second was Abijah, and they served at Beersheba. But his sons did not follow his ways. They turned aside after dishonest gain and accepted bribes and perverted justice.
>
> So all the elders of Israel gathered together and came to Samuel at Ramah. They said to him, "You are old, and your sons do not follow your ways; now appoint a king to lead us, such as all the other nations have."
>
> But when they said, "Give us a king to lead us," this displeased Samuel; so he prayed to the LORD. And the LORD told him: "Listen to all that the people are saying to you; it is not you they have rejected, but they have rejected me as their king. As

they have done from the day I brought them up out of Egypt until this day, forsaking me and serving other gods, so they are doing to you. Now listen to them; but warn them solemnly and let them know what the king who will reign over them will claim as his rights."

Samuel warned Israel what would happen when she received a king. This king would make their sons and daughters his servants, whether soldiers in his army or attendants in his court. He would tax the people and enslave them when they couldn't pay. Eventually Israel would once again cry out for relief—this time from the very king *they* asked for. But God would not listen (1 Samuel 8.10-18).

Basically, Samuel warned that Israel would again find herself in Egypt—this time an "Egypt" of her own making. But notice what they said next: *"No! We want a king over us. **Then we will be like all the other nations"*** (1 Samuel 8.19-20). Their response reveals the deep tragedy of this entire episode. The one nation God called to be holy—set apart, unique, *different*—wanted to be just like everyone else. They reject God as their king and foolishly demand an earthly substitute. The kingdoms of the world have co-opted the kingdom of God.

So God accepted their rejection and gave them a king so they could be like everyone else.

Once again hitting fast-forward, Israel's first king Saul—though incredibly tall and handsome—proved fearful and disobedient to God. Eventually God appointed David, who turned out to be the greatest of Israel's kings, as Saul's successor. The biblical books 1 and 2 Samuel tell of David's exploits—both positive and negative—and after more soap opera-like family drama, his son Solomon assumed the throne. God even let Solomon build a Temple in Jerusalem for God's presence to dwell, though in doing so Solomon fulfilled Samuel's negative prophecies about taxation and slave labor. He also built himself an even more impressive palace across the street! After Solomon's death the kingdom split in two—north ("Israel" or Samaria) and south ("Judah")—and from here things mostly turned from bad to worse. The northern kingdom never had a good king, and you can count all the good southern kings on one hand. During this time God raised up prophets like Elijah, Elisha,

Isaiah, Jeremiah, and Amos to call God's people and her rulers to faithfulness. For the most part, however, their messages were ignored (or worse), so eventually God did what he promised he would do if his "treasured possession" turned every which way but up.

Act III, Scene IV: God abandoned Israel into exile but promised future restoration

In 722 BC, Assyria stormed the northern kingdom and took Israel captive. (You can read the story in 2 Kings 17.) Less than 150 years later, the southern kingdom met a similar fate at the hands of the new world superpower — Babylon (2 Kings 25). When these foreign powers overtook Israel and Judah, they dispersed God's people throughout their empires and infiltrated Israel's land with captured folks from other areas. God's people found themselves in *exile*, cast away from their own land and seemingly abandoned by the God who loved them.

Inevitably they wondered what had happened, and God's prophets were ready with the not-so-great news. Israel's exile was punishment for her sins. Check out a few examples from 2 Kings 17.5-8 and 24.2-4, Amos 2.6-8, and Jeremiah 5.19, 26-29: *Exile as Punishment*

The king of Assyria invaded the entire land, marched against Samaria and laid siege to it for three years. In the ninth year of Hoshea, the king of Assyria captured Samaria [the northern kingdom] *and deported the Israelites to Assyria. He settled them in Halah, in Gozan on the Habor River and in the towns of the Medes. All this took place because the Israelites had sinned against the LORD their God, who had brought them up out of Egypt from under the power of Pharaoh king of Egypt. They worshiped other gods and followed the practices of the nations the LORD had driven out before them, as well as the practices that the kings of Israel had introduced.*

The LORD sent Babylonian, Aramean, Moabite and Ammonite raiders against him to destroy Judah, in accordance with the word of the LORD proclaimed by his servants the prophets. Surely these things happened to Judah according to the LORD's command, in order to remove them from his presence because of the sins of Manasseh and all he had done, including the

29

shedding of innocent blood. For he had filled Jerusalem with innocent blood, and the LORD was not willing to forgive.

This is what the LORD says: "For three sins of Israel, even for four, I will not relent. They sell the innocent for silver, and the needy for a pair of sandals. They trample on the heads of the poor as on the dust of the ground and deny justice to the oppressed. Father and son use the same girl and so profane my holy name. They lie down beside every altar on garments taken in pledge. In the house of their god they drink wine taken as fines."

"When the people ask, 'Why has the Lord our God done all this to us?' you will tell them, 'As you have forsaken me and served foreign gods in your own land, so now you will serve foreigners in a land not your own.' . . . Among my people are the wicked who lie in wait like men who snare birds and like those who set traps to catch people. Like cages full of birds, their houses are full of deceit; they have become rich and powerful and have grown fat and sleek. Their evil deeds have no limit; they do not seek justice. They do not promote the case of the fatherless; they do not defend the just cause of the poor. Should I not punish them for this?" declares the LORD. "Should I not avenge myself on such a nation as this?"

You get the point. Thanks to sins ranging from sexual infidelity to shedding innocent blood to economic injustice against the poor, God abandoned his people into captivity under pagan kingdoms.

This harsh word of judgment does not, however, end our story. As we've seen before, mercy gives way to judgment and God's faithfulness — not to mention his resourcefulness — knows no limit. He promised to bless the world through Abraham's family, and he always keeps his promises — even if it meant he'd have to finish the job himself! Woven into the prophetic oracles we also find messages of hope, words of future deliverance, and promises of restoration. To quote just one example, listen to God's promises through the prophet Micah (4.6-8):

"In that day," declares the LORD, "I will gather the lame; I will assemble the exiles and those I have brought to grief. I will

make the lame my remnant, those driven away a strong nation. The LORD will rule over them in Mount Zion from that day and forever. As for you, watchtower of the flock, stronghold of Daughter Zion, the former dominion will be restored to you; kingship will come to Daughter Jerusalem."

On promises like this Israel staked her belief that God would not abandon her forever.

THE STORY, JESUS, AND US

God's story finds its climax in Jesus

What does this story have to do with Jesus? It was the story he grew up hearing, so much so that he likely knew most of it by heart (and in more detail than I've depicted here). This story shaped his imagination, his beliefs about God, his hopes and dreams. No doubt it was in part as he reflected on this story that Jesus came to understand his unique calling in relation to it. It was, after all, a story in search of resolution. And as we can see from the far side, Jesus is the climax the story was looking for. Jesus is the center. He is the direction the story was headed all along. Our devotion to Jesus demands our attention to this story, just as our tending to the story sharpens our devotion to Jesus.

Here we find an answer to our next question: What does this story have to do with *us*? In terms of our goal to find the true Jesus, the story protects us from many misunderstandings of what Jesus came to do. To begin with, the story reminds us that God seeks to restore and renew creation's original purpose of being the realm over which he perfectly and lovingly reigns. Consequently, God's mission has never been to destroy the earth and take his favorite folks off to another more "spiritual" place. Why would God destroy his own kingdom? Creation will not be demolished. It will be redeemed.

Speaking of God's favorite folks, the story won't let us forget that the chosen ones aren't chosen for their own sake. On the contrary, they (or we) were chosen for the sake of the entire world. Sure they were blessed, but precisely to be a blessing. God absolutely called them out from among all peoples, but He did so in order to call those people back in. If we forget this truth, we will not succeed in the task God has given us. We don't exist for

31

ourselves, but for those who are on the outside—far from God, exiled in bondage to the consequences of their decisions, waiting for a message of hope, deliverance, and restoration.

The bottom line is this: Jesus didn't drop out of heaven unanticipated or unannounced. He was the centerpiece of God's centuries-long mission to redeem creation and its inhabitants from corruption. If we want to see Jesus, we must learn to view him through the lens this particular story provides. Otherwise we'll find that our lens is actually a mirror, and our vision of Jesus is little more than our own reflection.

Two

WHAT DID PEOPLE WANT FROM JESUS?

Our goal in this book is to look closely at Jesus as a real person. He's more than a myth, an icon, or a fun story for kids to believe in. He was and is a real human being. In classic theological language, we're exploring his "humanity." But the humanity of Jesus isn't just a generic category. Jesus came as a specific human being into a specific world, so paying close attention to that world will sharpen our vision of who he is.

Think about how certain historical figures can't be understood apart from their context. In the last chapter we mentioned Martin Luther King, Jr. Can you imagine trying to make sense of his life—or people such as Rosa Parks, John M. Perkins, or John F. Kennedy—without paying attention to the mid-20th century American struggle for civil rights? Or attempting to understand folks like George Washington, John and Abigail Adams, or General Cornwallis apart from any knowledge of early American history leading up to the Revolutionary War? We might discover a few facts here and memories there, but they'd be like individual pieces of a jigsaw puzzle with no box-lid to tell us how it all fits together.

Obviously we're doing a bit of history in this chapter, which some of you will love, others will hate, and still others won't care much one way or another. If this will discourage you from continuing with the rest of the book, skip this chapter and come back to it later. For those who feel up to it, however, I'm confident your vision of Jesus will be enriched!

GREAT EXPECTATIONS

Most of us don't think twice about calling Jesus "Jesus *Christ*." We probably haven't given it much thought, and we may even assume that "Christ" is Jesus' last name. "Jesus Christ" rolls off the tongue like John Smith or Brandon Beard. It's just a name, first and last. But with Jesus this actually isn't true. Much more than a name, in fact, "Christ" is a title that comes from the Greek word *Christos* and the Hebrew word *Mashiach* or "Messiah." Like any title, "Christ" communicates something significant about the person in question. (For instance, not everyone answers to "Doctor" or "President" or "Mom.") In their various languages the words for Messiah mean "anointed one" and label someone who has been anointed or commissioned for a particular task. In Hebrew history, prophets, priests, and especially kings were considered anointed by God in this special way.

Calling someone "Messiah" creates certain expectations about who a person is and what they have come to do. When Jesus showed up acting like a Messiah and not correcting those who called him a Messiah, he knowingly evoked the revolutionary hopes and dreams of ordinary first century Jews. When he traveled around the countryside like a campaigning politician announcing and enacting the arrival of God's kingdom, he addressed the unrest of a community weary of bondage and eagerly awaiting redemption.

In this chapter we'll talk about first century expectations of Jesus, but first let's take a quick look at our own. We all desire and, whether we admit it or not, *expect* certain things from Jesus. We believe that to some extent we can reliably predict what he would think, say, or do. And when he doesn't do what we expect, we find ourselves disappointed, hurt, maybe even angry.

Below is a list of about twenty questions to dig a little deeper on this point. Just to warn you, some of them are silly, others controversial, still others just plain weird. How would *you* answer each of the following questions:

- Was Jesus more likely to laugh or cry?
- Would being in financial debt cause Jesus concern?
- Does Jesus often feel frustrated with people and institutions?

- Would Jesus enjoy watching the Super Bowl?
- Does Jesus think marriage is old-fashioned and should be done away with?
- Could Jesus easily inject some life into a rather dull party?
- Would Jesus stay in the background on social occasions?
- Does Jesus pay close attention to detail?
- Would Jesus drive a BMW (or a Benz, Lexus, Bentley, Maserati, etc)?
- Did Jesus often feel alone and misunderstood?
- Does Jesus think it's better to follow society's rules than go one's own way?
- Would Jesus enjoy being part of your church?
- Would Jesus ever kill someone (such as in war or self-defense or to defend innocent people)?
- Does Jesus think abortion is acceptable in extreme circumstances?
- Would Jesus ever vote to legalize homosexual marriage?
- Did Jesus struggle to understand his purpose in life?
- Would Jesus have raised his hands in worship?
- Is Jesus often suspicious of people's motives?
- Is Jesus often annoyed by people's stupidity?
- Would Jesus consider himself a conservative/Republican?
- Would Jesus consider himself a liberal/Democrat?
- Would Jesus allow people into heaven who never had a chance to hear the gospel?
- How would Jesus exercise the power to stop bad things from happening to good people?

For the moment the point has nothing to do with whether your opinions are right, wrong, or ridiculous.[1] The point is that we all

---

[1] I encourage you to work back through the questions with yourself as the subject and then compare both sets of answers. I got the idea for this "quiz" from a similar one you can find in *The Blue Parakeet* by Scot McKnight (Grand Rapids: Zondervan, 2008).

already believe certain things about what Jesus is like—what he loves or hates, what he prefers and values, what he's doing or trying to do. All sorts of factors have shaped these beliefs, including our own personality, past history, friendships, reading list, and current life situation. In all these ways and many more, Jesus faces countless expectations from us today, some of them good and others not so much. In this chapter, by digging into the expectations people projected onto Jesus in his own day, we might learn a few things about our own.

THE WORLD OF JESUS

In order to get our hands around something as large and complex as "the world of Jesus," we'll organize our thoughts according to three key questions: (1) What was the problem in Jesus' world? (2) What did first century Jews want God to do about it? (3) What did they think they could do to compel God to act?

QUESTION ONE: WHAT WAS THE PROBLEM?

In a word, the problem was Rome. For those who knew their Israelite history and daily experienced the underside of empire, Rome was the new Egypt: the evil idolatrous oppressor laying unbearable burdens on God's chosen people.

Rome essentially moved in and took over in 63 BC. That year the Roman general Pompey came to town to resolve some internal disputes and, after a three-month siege of the Temple and the Jewish troops stationed there, annexed Israel's homeland. This ended the only century of independence Israel had known in the past 700 years. Soon thereafter Rome appointed a family of client kings to rule the area, which means they were "kings of the Jews" who actually worked for and with the Romans. Their family name was Herod, and we read about many of them in Scripture. The first King Herod took about three years to defeat Jewish guerilla warfare and establish Rome's powerbase there in Jerusalem. A few decades later in 4 BC this Herod died, leaving the throne temporarily vacant.

While various descendants of King Herod appealed to Rome to let them fill the power vacuum, mayhem ensued back home.

Among the many events that took place during these politically charged days and weeks, one Roman politician stole a load of money from the Temple treasury. About the same time a young rebel leader named Judas — whose dad Herod had previously murdered — gathered popular support in Galilee, attacked a Herodian fortress in a city called Sepphoris, and hijacked a bunch of weapons in order to fight for independence. (The Bible mentions this guy in Acts 5.37.)

Uprisings like this went on for some time, at least until the Roman General Varus arrived. In addition to burning towns and searching the hill country to snuff out rebel factions, Varus also once crucified 2000 Jews at the same time. Yes, you read that sentence correctly — *2000* crucifixions in one flex of imperial muscle. Another Roman general named Titus gathered rebels and put to death about 500 Jewish rebels every day in similar fashion. It got to the point that, as first century Jewish historian Josephus put it, "Space could not be found for the crosses nor crosses for the bodies."[2] Crucifixion's intimidation factor alone proved uniquely valuable to Rome, leaving no doubt that those who cross Rome will eventually hang on Roman crosses.

It was really bad. And while the Jews certainly weren't faultless in every instance, it's difficult to criticize their passion for freedom. While Rome famously expanded her empire under the rubric of *Pax Romana* ("Roman peace"), this mantra failed to match the experience of many subject peoples, in our case particularly the Jews. Like Egypt so long ago, Rome financially exploited most of her subjects. So economic factors also fed such reckless rebellion.

Let's imagine ourselves in a typical scenario. We're a Jewish family who has owned land for centuries — not a massive plot, but enough to keep the grandkids fed and the bills paid. Then the Romans move in and do what the Romans always do — they tax us along with all the other Jewish households. Taxation served many functions within the empire, including financing the empire's building projects and sustaining the luxury of its main

---

[2] Quoted in Shane Claiborne and Chris Haw, *Jesus for President* (Grand Rapids: Zondervan, 2008). The original quote can be found in Josephus, *Jewish War* 5.449-51.

cities (even if it meant poverty for everyone else).[3] At first this might not present much of a problem, at least until a bad crop season. But the thing about taxes is that they must always be paid! And when they wouldn't be, because at times they couldn't be, our family would sell off a portion of our land to the Romans—or rather their representatives the "tax collectors"—in order to make up the difference. Bit by bit *our* land would become *their* land, until we eventually became slaves on what used to be our own property.

As you might guess, such debt enslavement didn't win Rome many friends among occupied peoples like the Jews. To make matters worse, some of the Israelites' own people were colluding with this idolatrous, oppressive, God-dishonoring enemy. When oppressors take over a new area, they always find willing helpers from within the home culture, and there were leaders within Israel had happily accepted this role. In Jesus' day, three groups stand out in this regard.

I already mentioned the first: "tax collectors." We meet numerous tax collectors in the Gospels. Even Matthew, a disciple of Jesus and Gospel author, had been a tax collector before Jesus called him to leave everything behind and follow him. Tax collectors like Matthew were hated for a couple reasons. One was simply that they worked for the Romans. Maybe tax collectors figured they were making the best of a bad situation, but most Jews didn't share their perspective. To the majority of Jewish folks, they were traitors. Second, the way tax collectors made a living was by adding to the tax amount. What they charged above and beyond the regulated minimum became their income. Coming back to our imagined example above, these would be the people knocking on our family door asking for money they know we don't have. If you knew that some of your own people (a) were working for those who had recently enslaved you and were taxing you do death, and (b) were making a fine salary by

---

[3] Slave labor also helped, as the Jews knew all too well. This was yet another way their experience under Roman rule recalled their days in Egypt. One of the great Roman towns in Israel's land was Sepphoris, which King Herod built on the backs—not to mention the taxes—of Galileans (folks from the north where Jesus lived). We'll never know for sure, but it's even possible that as a child Jesus experienced some of these imperial building projects firsthand.

charging you above and beyond the normal requirements, you'd probably hate them too.

Second, when the Gospels talk about "the rich" people, they often have in mind landowners who profited from hardworking Jewish folks' difficult times. They might not be collecting cash for the enemy *per se*, but they certainly were benefiting from their poorer neighbors' hard times. This exploitation imitated the circumstances Nehemiah had encountered a few centuries earlier (Nehemiah 5.1-8):

> *Now the men and their wives raised a great outcry against their fellow Jews. Some were saying, "We and our sons and daughters are numerous; in order for us to eat and stay alive, we must get grain."*
>
> *Others were saying, "We are mortgaging our fields, our vineyards and our homes to get grain during the famine."*
>
> *Still others were saying, "We have had to borrow money to pay the king's tax on our fields and vineyards. Although we are of the same flesh and blood as our fellow Jews and though our children are as good as theirs, yet we have to subject our sons and daughters to slavery. Some of our daughters have already been enslaved, but we are powerless, because our fields and our vineyards belong to others."*
>
> *When I heard their outcry and these charges, I was very angry. I pondered them in my mind and then accused the nobles and officials. I told them, "You are charging your own people interest!" So I called together a large meeting to deal with them and said: "As far as possible, we have bought back our fellow Jews who were sold to the Gentiles. Now you are selling your own people, only for them to be sold back to us!" They kept quiet, because they could find nothing to say.*

Many Jews in Jesus' day were looking for someone like Nehemiah to come along and put an end to such offensive practices within the family of God—a family, remember, who was called to be distinct among the nations not least for taking special care of their poor folks.

As had so often been the case in her history, Israel's appointed leaders had traded in their God-given responsibilities for the bright red fruit of money and power. Jewish rebels despised traitorous Jewish leaders—especially those who ran the Temple—as angrily as they did the Romans. Many saw no difference at all between the two. Indeed, Temple leaders and chief priestly families comprise the third group cooperating with Rome. Among the many reproaches prophets delivered to self-serving priests and Temple rulers, take a look at these words from Micah 3.1-3, 9-12 (see also Isaiah 1.21-23; 56.10-12; Ezekiel 34.1-6):

> *Then I said, "Listen, you leaders of Jacob, you rulers of Israel. Should you not embrace justice, you who hate good and love evil; who tear the skin from my people and the flesh from their bones; who eat my people's flesh, strip off their skin and break their bones in pieces; who chop them up like meat for the pan, like flesh for the pot?"*

> *"Hear this, you leaders of Jacob, you rulers of Israel, who despise justice and distort all that is right; who build Zion with bloodshed, and Jerusalem with wickedness. Her leaders judge for a bribe, her priests teach for a price, and her prophets tell fortunes for money. Yet they look for the LORD's support and say, 'Is not the LORD among us? No disaster will come upon us.' Therefore because of you, Zion will be plowed like a field, Jerusalem will become a heap of rubble, the temple hill a mound overgrown with thickets."*

The evils Micah denounced during Israel's years under Assyria's thumb mirrored the problems Jesus' contemporaries faced under Rome's. Good prophet that he was, Jesus castigated Temple money-makers for turning God's sacred place into a "den of robbers" (Matthew 21.12-17; Mark 11.15-19; Luke 19.45-48; John 2.13-16). In particular he went after those who sold doves, which was the offering of poor folks like Jesus' parents (see Leviticus 5.7 and 12.8, as well as Luke 2.22-24). When Jewish rebels seized control of the Temple in 66 AD in one of the last big efforts to overthrow Rome, they immediately burned the tax records. This powerfully demonstrated how fed up many Jewish folks were with the financial dealings of their Temple leaders.

Predicaments like this were hardly new for the Jews. As you may remember, enslavement in one form or another had characterized their lives for centuries. Take a look at their history of bondage in the timeline below.

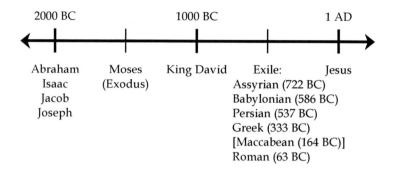

Notice the fourth column in particular. From the Assyrians down to the Romans — with the exception of a single one-hundred-year period — God's people were ruled by someone other than God. Note also the familiar title given to this time period as a whole: *exile*.[4] Israel's problem wasn't just that she was under Rome's reign, but that Rome's rule recalled her unfaithfulness to God's rule. Remember that Israel's exile was punishment for her disobedience to God's covenant, and as such Rome's presence was a constant reminder of the distance God maintained on account of her rebellion. As long as Rome ruled over her, she was forced to stare at idolatrous emblems and statues in the heart of God's great city (Jerusalem) and Temple. These served as continual reminders that the world was not as it should be.

QUESTION TWO: WHAT DID THEY WANT GOD TO DO ABOUT IT?

No one would rest easy in such tense and offensive conditions for long, least of all a people who believed they were to play a special role in the One True God's mission to redeem creation.

---

[4] Some of you may be thinking, "I thought Israel returned from exile. Isn't that what the stories of Ezra and Nehemiah are all about?" That is true to an extent, but the many acts of rebellion from the time of Jesus, as well as much of the Jewish literature written then, prove that most Jews still knew the world was not as it should be. And "exile" was one of the ways they labeled this problem. Only *some* of them returned to the Land, and even those who had continued to live under someone else's rule.

God had liberated them from a similar predicament before and he could do it again. In many ways they hoped for exactly that: a *new exodus* that would once again free them from oppression. They looked forward to a time (hopefully soon!) when people would no longer say, "*As surely as the LORD lives, who brought the Israelites up out of Egypt,*" but rather, "*As surely as the LORD lives, who brought the descendants of Israel up out of the land of the north and out of all the countries where he had banished them*" (Jeremiah 23.7-8). In other words, people would no longer talk about the original exodus because this second exodus would take its place as God's most newsworthy feat.

Their hope for a new liberation had four basic dimensions.

First, the Israelites wanted God to *rescue* them from oppression by destroying the Romans for their arrogance and sins. This comes as no great surprise considering that Israel had plenty of ammunition in their Scriptures indicating God's ability to wipe out an empire with little more than a whisper (Psalm 46.6-7). Once again they hoped the kingdom of God would overthrow the kingdoms of the world. When they read passages such as Daniel 7, Psalm 2, and Joel 3, along with dozens of others, they looked forward to Rome's descent.

Second, they wanted God to *rebuild* the Temple and *rule* the world from its throne. Note, for example, Amos 9.11: "*In that day I will restore David's fallen shelter. I will repair its broken walls and restore its ruins, and will rebuild it as it used to be.*" Many times the prophets combine these two themes of God destroying her enemies and rebuilding the Temple (also known as "Mount Zion"): *In that day the LORD will punish the powers in the heavens above and the kings on the earth below. They will be herded together like prisoners bound in a dungeon; they will be shut up in prison and be punished after many days. The moon will be dismayed, the sun ashamed; for the LORD Almighty will reign on Mount Zion and in Jerusalem, and before its elders – with great glory* (Isaiah 24.21-23). Other Scriptures expressing this Temple-centered hope include Micah 4.1-5 and Ezekiel 40-48.

Third, they leaned on God's promises to *re-gather* exiled Israelites for renewed enjoyment of God's blessings in the Promised Land. Of the many prophecies we could examine, one contains one of the Bible's most popular verses.[5] Some of you may even have it hanging on your wall! However, you might not know that it wasn't originally about God's care in a general sense, but rather his specific promise to re-gather Israel from exile. In this light take a look at Jeremiah 29.10-14:

> "I will come to you and fulfill my good promise to bring you back to this place. For I know the plans I have for you," declares the LORD, "plans to prosper you and not to harm you, plans to give you hope and a future. Then you will call on me and come and pray to me, and I will listen to you. You will seek me and find me when you seek me with all your heart. I will be found by you," declares the LORD, "and will bring you back from captivity. I will gather you from all the nations and places where I have banished you," declares the LORD, "and will bring you back to the place from which I carried you into exile."

The *hope and future* that God promised was about life on the other side of exile. Jesus' contemporaries eagerly awaited this prophecy's fulfillment.

Fourth and finally, God's people anticipated the *resurrection* of faithful Israelites into a golden age of justice and peace. Birthed from texts such as Daniel 12.1-3 and expressed for instance in Martha's words to Jesus in John 11.24 — "I know [Lazarus] will rise again in the resurrection at the last day" — Jewish hope for resurrection arose as she came to understand God's ultimate plan for restoring life to a dying creation. With the exception of a few dissenters, Jews in Jesus' day believed in and hoped for resurrection as the one event that would most clearly mark the complete fulfillment of God's promises to Israel. All God's faithful ones would be raised together to live forever in the world as God intended it.[6]

These four dimensions — rescuing the Jews from oppression, rebuilding the Temple, re-gathering exiled Israelites, and

---

[5] Jeremiah 29.11 came second to John 3.16. "The 100 most-read Bible verses at Biblegateway.com" <http://www.biblegateway.com/blog/2009/05/the-100-most-read-bible-verses-at-biblegatewaycom> Accessed February 19, 2011.

[6] In addition to the texts mentioned above, we see this belief stated or assumed in other writings of the time such as 2 Maccabees 7.11; 12.43-45; Mishnah 10.1.

resurrecting the faithful—together make up what people would have *wanted* and even *expected* from Jesus as he traveled around the Holy Land proclaiming, teaching, and enacting the kingdom of God. When they heard him say that God's kingdom had come, those who hoped in him believed these things would take place very soon.

Think of these hopes like an atom. The nucleus is what Jesus calls "the kingdom of God," around which everything else revolves. And the orbiting electrons represent what hoping for God's kingdom looked like on the ground.

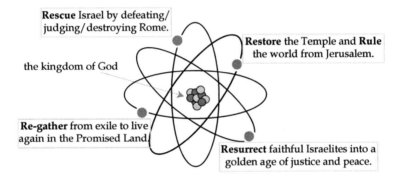

Rescue Israel by defeating/judging/destroying Rome.

the kingdom of God

Restore the Temple and **Rule** the world from Jerusalem.

Re-gather from exile to live again in the Promised Land.

Resurrect faithful Israelites into a golden age of justice and peace.

Think back to our definition of God's kingdom: the realm over which God rules, where his name is properly honored and his will is promptly done. If you were to ask Jesus' family and friends, "What in God's name does that look like?" they just might pull out a napkin and draw something like this. (Okay, not possible. But they'd say something like what our atom depicts!) This would be their *new exodus* (Isaiah 14.1; Jeremiah 23.3-8) that signaled a *new covenant* (Jeremiah 31.31-34; Hosea 2.14-18) and ushered in nothing less than *new creation* (Isaiah 65.17-25).

Not to belabor the point, but let's explore one more way of picturing all this—a timeline. Many Jews divided history into two sections: this age and the age to come; creation and new creation; the age of flesh and the age of Spirit. Here's how they might have drawn *this* on a napkin:

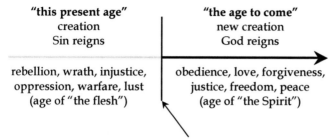

"this present age"	"the age to come"
creation	new creation
Sin reigns	God reigns

| rebellion, wrath, injustice, oppression, warfare, lust (age of "the flesh") | obedience, love, forgiveness, justice, freedom, peace (age of "the Spirit") |

The "day of the Lord" when God leads Israel in a new exodus ushering in new creation: the wicked are defeated, the Temple is restored, the exiles are gathered, and the righteous are resurrected (perhaps through a liberator like Moses / king like David)

These two ages would be separated by an event (or set of events) the prophets often referred to as "the last days" or "the day of the LORD." On this day (or days), whether on his own or through some sort of *Messiah*, God would do exactly what our atom above maps out: rescue, rebuild, restore, and resurrect. (To see one last example that pulls most of this together into one place, check out Micah 4.)

Among other festivals and holy days, the Jews' annual Passover celebration expressed exactly this matrix of memory and hope. Rome even filled Jerusalem with extra soldiers during the week of Passover because hope for revolution filled the air! This is also, to say it one more time, precisely what people would have expected when Jesus arrived on the scene declaring that time was up and God's kingdom had come.

QUESTION THREE: HOW COULD THEY COMPEL GOD TO ACT?

Don't let the above analysis fool you though. Jewish expectations were hardly uniform. Different groups and factions responded to the Roman crisis in four distinct and often incompatible ways.

Option #1: Compromise

For starters, not all Jews believed Rome presented a crisis. On the contrary, some viewed Roman rule as a wonderful (or at least salvageable) opportunity. Think in particular of the tax collectors, rich folks, Temple leaders, and priestly families mentioned above. Additional groups named in the Gospels to include here are chief priests, Sadducees, and Herodians. In a way they lived by the common motto: "If life gives you lemons, make lemonade." In this case, the lemons were Roman occupation and lemonade was getting what you could within the current system. They were the "realists" of their day. To justify their accommodations, they rejected all but the first five books of what we call the Old Testament—can't have those pesky prophets getting in the way of gaining money and power! They also rejected revolutionary doctrines like the resurrection (see Mark 12.18 and Acts 23.8).

Option #2: Withdraw

The corrupt compromise in option one provoked a second reaction: withdraw. Move out to the wilderness and wait for God to destroy not only Rome, but the unfaithful in Israel as well. In the last century, archaeologists discovered the *Dead Sea Scrolls*, a collection of writings from a group called "Essenes" who camped out at a place known as Qumran. They believed that God had already restored his true people in their own community, and that it was only a matter of time before his harsh judgment revealed this truth to the world. Instead of making lemonade, groups like the Essenes might have said, "If life gives you lemons, then go somewhere else, plant oranges, and wait for God to strike the lemon trees with lightning."

Option #3: Fight

A third group found not only widespread support, but also many willing participants. We've already talked about "Judas the Galilean," who was one among dozens of young zealots who believed God was waiting for his people to work up enough faith to challenge the mighty Romans. They were inspired by ancient Hebrew stories such as Gideon vs. the Midianites, Hezekiah vs. the Assyrian king Sennacherib, and of course David vs. Goliath (Judges 6-7, 2 Chronicles 32.1-23, and 1 Samuel 17). These passionate rebels often used revolutionary violence at great personal cost, trusting all the while in God's ability to overcome ridiculous odds. One particular gang called themselves "Sicarii," named for the small curved-blade daggers they would carry hidden in their cloaks to kidnap, intimidate, and even assassinate

Roman authorities and Jewish collaborators. Freedom-fighters such as Judas the Galilean and the Sicarii lived by a different (some might say simpler) creed than the above two options: "If life gives you lemons, kill the farmers and plant oranges." This, they believed, would move God to act on their behalf and once again miraculously defeat the "Goliath" that was Rome. (In fact, forty years after Jesus, the Jewish people did engage in widespread revolt against Rome, leading to the eventual destruction of the Temple in 70 AD. After one more attempt around 135 AD, Judaism for the most part abandoned hope for revolution and focused more and more on studying Torah.)

Option #4: Purify

Lastly we have the Pharisees. While the word "Pharisee" has become a putdown synonymous with hypocrisy and the worst kind of religious bigot, the Pharisees of Jesus' day were highly respected almost to the point of being popular heroes. Like the zealous freedom-fighters, Pharisees hoped and worked for revolution. They too sought no less than complete freedom from Roman rule, though their method for securing this freedom differed a bit. They understood quite well why God had abandoned them into exile. Since sin was the problem, radical obedience to God's Law was the only adequate solution. Perhaps God would see their devotion, forgive their transgressions, and save them. They went so far in this pursuit that they not only obeyed the Law itself, but also hundreds of oral traditions compiled over the years. These rabbinic teachings aimed to move them so far away from disobedience to God that angering him would be impossible. In particular, they separated themselves from everything profane and unclean, whether foods, cultural customs, or people. Their lemon-motto would be something like this: "If life gives you lemons, it's because you deserve lemons. Root out all wickedness and impurities from among you, and *then* God will give you oranges."

WHAT DO *WE* WANT FROM JESUS?

Ultimately none of them got it right, or what they got right was overshadowed by what they ignored or got wrong. They missed the point in part because they forgot Israel's calling as the world's true light, the conduit through which God's *blessing* would reach all people—even their enemies. So Jesus called all of them to repent. To "repent" means to change your mind, to transform how you think and therefore how you live. In other words, drop your agenda with its faulty vision of God and God's kingdom, and accept Jesus' definitions and program.

Trying to fit Jesus' vision of God's kingdom into these predetermined molds would be like sewing a patch of unshrunk cloth onto an already laundered quilt. Or pouring unfermented wine into previously expanded wineskins. The quilt would be torn to shreds. The wineskins would burst. In order to find themselves fit for this kingdom, as Jesus once told a Jewish religious leader, they must break clean and start fresh. Nothing less than a *new birth* was necessary to purge their longings and sanctify their imaginations. (See Mark 2.18-22; John 3.1-8.)

Jesus didn't fit into their wineskins or quilts or boxes, and he won't fit into ours either. We might even say Jesus has an aversion to boxes—or, as we're calling them here, expectations.

Even though we find ourselves on the far side—of Jesus ministry, death, and resurrection; of the inspired composition and collection of the Gospels as sacred Scripture; of centuries filled with beautiful successes and horrendous failures—expectations haven't become any less dangerous. We know what Jesus said and did, or at least we can know if we read our Bibles. But availability breeds a false familiarity that sometimes shields us from the surprising truth of this strange prophet from Nazareth.

Good first century Jewish folks wanted certain things from their Messiah, and their desires and expectations caused most of them to miss Jesus. We'd best be careful lest ours do the very same thing.

Three

WHAT DID JESUS COME HERE TO DO?

I can't think of a more important question than the one we're asking in this book: Who is Jesus? And I know of no better way to position ourselves for a faithful answer than by asking another question: What did Jesus do?

Jesus never wrote an autobiography or sat down for an interview as one of the year's most interesting celebrities. All we have to verify his identity are a few inspired records of what he said and did during his brief sojourn on earth. Of course we also have our present experience of Jesus — he is very much alive, after all! — but experience often misleads as much as it illuminates (as experience itself teaches). And if what we think and say about Jesus today doesn't line up with what Jesus did during his time on earth, then we're not actually thinking and talking about Jesus. We're talking and thinking about something we have invented and decided to call "Jesus."

So far we've set ourselves up to hear the truth about Jesus. Now it's time to make this truth plain. We've been testing and tilling the soil, so to speak, and the time has come to plant our garden. Or to change the metaphor, we've been running sprints, repeating drills, and rehearsing the playbook, but the game is about to begin. The remaining chapters of this book will spell out different aspects of what Jesus came here to do.

One further clarification as we get going. In asking "What did Jesus do?" we certainly want to progress beyond the obvious answers: performed miracles and exorcisms, gathered disciples, taught the masses using parables, offended the religious and political authorities, got himself crucified, and so on. Our goal is not to compose a bullet-pointed list of all Jesus' words and actions; rather our goal is to discover how it all fits together. There's a difference between watching someone randomly roll dough, slice peppers, spread sauce, position pepperonis, and sprinkle cheese, and understanding that this person is making a pizza. What larger agenda makes sense of the specific actions we see Jesus perform again and again in the Scriptures?

PROCLAIMING AND ESTABLISHING GOD'S KINGDOM

As you've probably guessed by now, what pulls together all of Jesus' action and effort is something he most often called "the kingdom of God." No one who reads the Gospels closely can honestly deny that God's coming kingdom forms the center around which Jesus' entire ministry revolved. As we sketched out in the introduction, the first words Jesus spoke as he began his mission were, *"The time has come. The kingdom of God has come near. Repent and believe the good news!"* (Mark 1.14-15; also Matthew 4.17). When some folks tried to keep Jesus from leaving, he explained to them, *"I must proclaim the good news of the kingdom of God to the other towns also, because that is why I was sent"* (Luke 4.43). Did you catch that? The purpose for which God sent Jesus to earth was to proclaim the good news of the kingdom of God. This is why *Jesus traveled about from one town and village to another, proclaiming the good news of the kingdom of God* (Luke 8.1). Consequently he taught his followers to seek this kingdom of God above all else (Matthew 6.33), and likewise sent them out to proclaim it themselves (Luke 9.1-2, 61; also Matthew 10.5-8). The coming of God's kingdom forms the center of Jesus' most famous prayer (Matthew 6.9-10), clarifies the meaning of his miracles (Luke 11.20; Matthew 12.28), is the subject of his parables (Luke 8.9; also Matthew 13), and explains his strange and defenseless acceptance of suffering and death (John 18.36). Twice Matthew summarizes Jesus' ministry as *teaching in their synagogues, proclaiming the good news of the kingdom, and healing every disease and sickness among the people* (Matthew 4.23; 9.35). In all these ways and more, we see that Jesus came to declare and demonstrate the presence of the kingdom of God.

In the last two chapters, we learned a great deal about the long story of God's search for a kingdom recorded in the Old Testament. This story reminds us that God originally intended creation to mirror his heavenly kingdom on earth. He would accomplish this primarily through human beings as his kingdom-agents. But our original calling to reflect God's goodness got (and gets) derailed by our rebellious grasp for independent power. We'd rather set up our own kingdoms, thanks very much. The mess we made led God to initiate a program of redemption. God chose to rescue creation from corruption and bondage by making a covenant with a particular group of human beings. God would make this community—the family of Abraham, the people of Israel—a kingdom of priests and a holy nation. God's character would be revealed in them, and through them his blessing would reach out and grab hold of us all. By and large they failed, but in Jesus this community faithfully fulfilled its calling. He came to accomplish the task for which his people had been commissioned: To embody God's heavenly kingdom on earth and invite the rest of us into it. As such Jesus is the pinnacle of God's redemption of the entire world.

We also learned how first century Jews expected this story to resolve. They expected God to rescue them from the Romans through military conquest, rebuild his holy Temple and rule the world from its throne, re-gather his scattered children to live in the land he promised them, and resurrect all the faithful ones who had already died so they too could experience eternal life. In their minds, anyone who declared the coming of God's kingdom implied that these things would soon take place.

Jesus came to announce that God was finally establishing the kingdom he had been seeking since the beginning. To take it a step further, Jesus believed that God's kingdom was arriving in and through his own life and ministry. He is the kingdom-in-person—the story fulfilled, the world restored, the kingdom come. Jesus both claimed this in word and demonstrated it in action. Let's first take a look at what Jesus said.

Jesus claimed in various ways that his entry onto the world's stage marked the arrival of God's kingdom. To flesh this out we'll take a look at two incidents from the Gospel of Luke. In the first event Jesus goes public with the mission God sent him to accomplish, but let's first back up and get a bit of a running start.

The early chapters of Luke's Gospel consist of person after person witnessing about Jesus being the one God sent to fulfill his promises. First note how the angel Gabriel assures Mary that her virginal conception is from God: *"You will conceive and give birth to a son, and you are to call him Jesus. He will be great and will be called the Son of the Most High. The Lord God will give him the throne of his father David, and he will reign over Jacob's descendants forever; his kingdom will never end."* Then, after her relative Elizabeth confirms something special about this child (Luke 2.39-45), Mary herself sings: *"God has brought down rulers from their thrones but has lifted up the humble. He has filled the hungry with good things but has sent the rich away empty. He has helped his servant Israel, remembering to be merciful to Abraham and his descendants forever, just as he promised our ancestors"* (Luke 2.52-55). Jesus' actual birth is announced by an angel (who calls Jesus *Savior, Messiah,* and *Lord*) to shepherds hard at work, after which *a great company of the heavenly host appeared with the angel* and praised God for what he had done. Immediately the shepherds visit the child, and then go off to tell others what they had seen. When Mary and Joseph took Jesus to the Temple to be dedicated to the Lord, two more people joined the chorus of praise: Simeon, a righteous and devout man whom God promised would see the Messiah before he died, and the prophetess Anna who saw in Jesus *the redemption of Jerusalem* (Luke 2.25-38). All this is pretty high praise for a baby still wearing diapers.

Fast forwarding a bit, at the end of chapter three we find Jesus being baptized by his cousin John, who was sent to prepare the way for the Messiah. At this baptism, God himself audibly confirms Jesus as his Son (which, by the way, was among other things a way of calling Jesus his appointed king; see 2 Samuel 7.12-14; Psalm 2). Luke informs us Jesus was about thirty years old at this point. Jesus began his ministry by withdrawing to the desert for a forty-day fast, during which Satan tempted him three times to short circuit his calling as God's Son. Three times Jesus resists. Upon his return from the desert we find Jesus back home in Nazareth, and this is (finally!) the event where Jesus first publicly acknowledges what he's been sent to do.

It's the Sabbath day, which means we'll find Jesus in the synagogue worshiping, praying, and reading Torah with his Jewish family and friends. During these gatherings someone would unroll one of the Scripture scrolls and read from it, after which those assembled would enter a period of prayerful reflection, teaching, and discussion. (This is, for example, what we see in Acts 13.13ff.) On this occasion Jesus stood up to read and someone handed him a scroll inked with the words of Isaiah the prophet. Here is what happens next (Luke 4.17-21):

> *Unrolling it, he found the place where it is written: "The Spirit of the Lord is on me, because he has anointed me to proclaim good news to the poor. He has sent me to proclaim freedom for the prisoners and recovery of sight for the blind, to set the oppressed free, to proclaim the year of the Lord's favor."*
>
> *Then he rolled up the scroll, gave it back to the attendant and sat down. The eyes of everyone in the synagogue were fastened on him.*
>
> *He began by saying to them, "Today this scripture is fulfilled in your hearing."*

Imagine what it would have been like to be there! You have this young Jewish man who was born a few decades ago under peculiar circumstances, to say the least. You've heard the rumors and the stories, but you've never been quite sure if you buy it. He's nice enough, you figure, but the Messiah? Probably a bit of a stretch. Anyway, if he's going to make something happen he'd better get to it! So now you go to synagogue just like any other Sabbath, and lo and behold he's there! You watch him the whole time to see if anything about him has changed, anything that would indicate big plans. The time of Scripture reading comes, he stands up, and before you know it he has quoted a promise you've been dreaming about for longer than you can remember.

He sits down. Your eyes — like everyone else's — aren't even blinking, much less looking away. Then he says one sentence you know without a doubt you will never forget: *Today this Scripture is fulfilled in your hearing.*

This Scripture that Jesus claims to fulfill comes from Isaiah 61 and speaks directly to the hopes of Jesus' contemporaries. Its section of Isaiah overflows with the dreams and aspirations we've come to recognize: the rebuilding of Israel's cities (58.12; 60.10-12; 61.4), God triumphing over Israel's oppressors (58.14; 59.18-19; 60.14), scattered Jews returning from exile (60.4-9), and peace in the Holy Land (60.18). And in the actual words Jesus quotes, we read of one *anointed* by God to deliver his people from oppression to freedom, from blindness to sight, from poverty to abundance.[1] This was the gospel Jesus preached, a gospel Isaiah elsewhere declares to be news of God's victorious *reign*, that is, his kingdom (Isaiah 52.7-10). All this, Jesus said, had found fulfillment *today*, the day when Jesus officially began his work.

Our second passage from Luke's Gospel is much shorter and to the point:

> *Once, on being asked by the Pharisees when the kingdom of God would come, Jesus replied, "The coming of the kingdom of God is not something that can be observed, nor will people say, 'Here it is,' or 'There it is,' because the kingdom of God is in your midst."*

When asked when the kingdom would come, Jesus says, in effect, "Um, hello. God's kingdom is here, among you, in your midst. If you're looking at me, you're looking at the kingdom."[2] Jesus is saying the kingdom is wherever he is. Where Jesus is, there is God's kingdom.

---

[1] The word for "anointed" is the verb form of the noun translated "Christ" or "Messiah." Jesus was covertly claiming to be the Messiah.

[2] Some versions of the Bible translate Jesus' words as "the kingdom of God is within you," and many folks have interpreted Jesus as saying that God's kingdom was located within their hearts. No doubt this fits well with today's popular belief that to get in touch with God all we need to do is look within ourselves. But it's a bad translation that leads to an even worse theology. Jesus isn't saying that the kingdom hides within their hearts (or yours or mine). Among other problems, this interpretation totally ignores the fact that Jesus is talking to some of his fiercest antagonists. He hardly meant that God's kingdom resided within the hearts of those who opposed him.

Of course all this telling means nothing without backing it up. Anyone can claim that God is doing something special, but saying it and showing it are two different things.

Jesus' Actions: The Kingdom Demonstrated

Thankfully, in many ways Jesus fulfills the cliché, "Actions speak louder than words." Jesus not only claimed that in himself God's kingdom was alive and activated, he backed up his claim by healing the sick, casting out demons, restoring sight to the blind, calming the sea, bringing dead people back to life, and other likewise wondrous feats.

We typically call these mighty works "miracles," but the biblical word for them is "signs." As "signs" they point beyond themselves. They indicate that something else is going on. What do they point to? What do they signify is happening? Jesus himself provides the answer: *"If it is by the Spirit of God that I drive out demons, then the kingdom of God has come upon you"* (Matthew 12.28). In other words, his exorcisms point to the work of God's Spirit through Jesus, which indicates the presence of God's kingdom. Also recall Matthew's summaries we quoted above, which similarly associate Jesus' healings with God's kingdom: *Jesus went through all the towns and villages, teaching in their synagogues, proclaiming the good news of the kingdom and healing every disease and sickness* (Matthew 9.35; 4.23).

What's more, some of the Gospels' miracle stories hint that more is going on than initially meets the eye (as if what meets the eye isn't impressive enough!). Remember how the most important Old Testament event was God's liberation of Israel from slavery in Egypt? And remember how Jesus' people looked for a second exodus modeled on the first? Well, let's look again at the way Jesus explained the significance of his miracles, only this time we'll quote from the Gospel of Luke: *"If I drive out demons by the finger of God, then the kingdom of God has come upon you"* (Luke 11.20). It's basically the same statement as in Matthew, except Luke has replaced "Spirit of God" with "finger of God," which is strange because Luke usually talks about the Holy Spirit more than the other Gospel writers. He's obviously making a point, but what could that point be? The answer is in the original exodus story, which is the only place in the Old Testament we find the phrase "finger of God." It is used twice to describe God writing the Ten Commandments on stone tablets. But we're most interested in the third usage, because it has to do with the miracles Moses and Aaron performed as they confronted Pharaoh—the "signs" indicating God's sovereignty over Pharaoh and the gods of Egypt. Here's the quote from Exodus 8.16-20:

> Then the LORD said to Moses, "Tell Aaron, 'Stretch out your staff and strike the dust of the ground,' and throughout the land of Egypt the dust will become gnats." They did this, and when Aaron stretched out his hand with the staff and struck the dust of the ground, gnats came on people and animals. All the dust throughout the land of Egypt became gnats. But when the magicians tried to produce gnats by their secret arts, they could not.
>
> Since the gnats were on people and animals everywhere, the magicians said to Pharaoh, "This is the finger of God." But Pharaoh's heart was hard and he would not listen, just as the LORD had said.
>
> Then the LORD said to Moses, "Get up early in the morning and confront Pharaoh as he goes to the river and say to him, 'This is what the LORD says: Let my people go, so that they may worship me.'"

When Jesus refers to his kingdom-signs as energized *by the finger of God*, we can almost see the nervous jostling and hear the hushed whispers, "Did you hear that? You know where that comes from, don't you? That's exodus-talk!" Jesus' explanation signifies another liberation from bondage to evil. God was finally doing what he had promised for so long.[3]

---

[3] We might not think much of an allusion like this one, but Jewish people knew their Scriptures extremely well, and not because they *read* them often (very few people had their own copies) but because they *heard* them read weekly in synagogue. Their ears were tuned in to hints and clues such as this one, especially when the hints and clues recalled the most important story in their sacred writings. It would be like an American politician beginning a speech about racial reconciliation with the words, "Four score and seven years ago." Most of us recognize these words from Abraham Lincoln's Gettysburg Address, which celebrated the end of the Civil War and the institution of slavery.

One more thing and then we'll move on. Not only do Jesus' miracles signify a new exodus, they go one step further and actually anticipate new creation. His signs do more than simply show us the fact of God's kingdom. They also serve as windows into what God's kingdom looks like—creation restored to its original harmony, beauty, and peace. God's kingdom is a realm where seas are restored from chaos to stillness, where the blind receive sight, the mute speak, the lame walk, the sick are made well, the demons are expelled, and even the dead return to life (Matthew 8.23-27; 11.1-5). This is creation healed, renewed, redeemed. The world gone wrong has been made right. In these ways the miracles of Jesus—and in a larger sense, the life of Jesus as a whole—are glimpses of another world breaking through time and space to invade this one.

So we see that according to both Jesus' words and actions, he believed the kingdom of God was becoming a present reality on earth through his own life and work. There was and certainly still is a future dimension to God's kingdom, but part of this future was reaching across the timeline into the present.

Let me state the obvious, however: There is no such thing as a kingdom without citizens. It's like a team without players or an alliance without trusted friends. If no one acknowledges and lives within a king's rule, is the king really a king? Every kingdom requires a community to embody the reign of its king. Hope for God's coming kingdom was always tied to anticipation of Israel's full return from exile—in a word, her *restoration* as God's favored and faithful treasured possession.

RESTORING AND REFORMING GOD'S FAMILY

In this regard Jesus didn't wholly disappoint. Jesus wasn't satisfied with manifesting the kingdom through his own impressive deeds. He sought to establish its visibility by calling together a community of disciples to continue Israel's job of being the people through whom God would shine his light into a darkened world. The coming of God's kingdom implied the restoration of God's people for faithful completion of her task.

Many prophets promised that God would gather and restore a "remnant," meaning a group within Israel who would faithfully move God's mission forward. Certain elements of Jesus' ministry suggest that he saw himself renewing God's chosen people by assembling such a remnant. We'll briefly mention six in particular.

First, Jesus aligns himself with the ministry of his cousin John the Baptist (see Matthew 3.1-17; Mark 1.1-11; Luke 3.1-20; John 1.6-8, 15, 19-34). Even before he was born an angel predicted the following of John: *He will bring back many of the people of Israel to the Lord their God* (Luke 1.16; see also Luke 1.67-79). To this end, John denounced Israel's hypocrisy, called her to repentance, and urged penitent Israelites to be baptized as true "children of Abraham." John's ministry was about restoring God's true family in preparation for what God was about to do.

Second, one of the more surprising but consistent characteristics of Jesus' earthly ministry is that he focuses almost solely on his fellow Jews (Matthew 10.5-6; 15.21-28; see also Luke 1.54-55; 19.9-10). He once said that he *was sent only to the lost sheep of Israel*, which recalls prophecies of Israel's re-gathering such as Micah 2.12: *"I will surely gather all of you, Jacob; I will surely bring together the remnant of Israel. I will bring them together like sheep in a pen, like a flock in its pasture; the place will throng with people."* This exclusive dimension makes sense when you know what Jesus knew: In making a covenant with Israel, God committed himself to reaching the rest of us through her. Jesus definitely came to rescue you and me, but he did so by first restoring Abraham's family — the people God promised to save us through in the first place.

Third, in one of his most noteworthy early moves, Jesus chooses exactly twelve disciples to form the core of his movement (Mark 3.13-19; notice the repetition of "twelve" here and in Matthew 10.1-8):

Jesus went up on a mountainside and called to him those he wanted, and they came to him. He appointed twelve that they might be with him and that he might send them out to preach and to have authority to drive out demons. These are the twelve he appointed: Simon (to whom he gave the name Peter), James son of Zebedee and his brother John (to them he gave the name Boanerges, which means "sons of thunder"), Andrew, Philip, Bartholomew, Matthew, Thomas, James son of Alphaeus, Thaddaeus, Simon the Zealot and Judas Iscariot, who betrayed him.

The twelve apostles correspond to the twelve tribes of Israel (see Matthew 19.28; Luke 22.29-30). Interestingly enough, both ancient prophets and more contemporary Jewish writings include the re-establishment of the twelve tribes as part of Israel's renewal. Among the biblical prophets, no one emphasizes this more than Ezekiel when he talks about Israel's restoration: *This is what the Sovereign LORD says: "These are the boundaries of the land that you will divide among the twelve tribes of Israel as their inheritance, with two portions for Joseph. You are to divide it equally among them. Because I swore with uplifted hand to give it to your ancestors, this land will become your inheritance.* (47.13-14; see also 45.8 and all of chapters 47-48). Jesus' calling of the Twelve indicates that he believed God was restoring a faithful remnant in his own movement.

Fourth, in John 15 Jesus speaks of himself as a vine and his followers as his branches. Taken at face value the passage beautifully moves and instructs us, but it has even more to offer than we typically realize. One of the prophets' favorite ways of describing Israel's rise and fall was to compare her to a vine: *The vineyard of the LORD Almighty is the nation of Israel, and the people of Judah are the vines he delighted in* (Isaiah 5.7). In the exodus, God planted this vine and in exile uprooted it (Ezekiel 19.10-14; Isaiah 5.1-7; Jeremiah 2.21-22; 8.11-13; Hosea 10.1-2). In turn the vine's recovery represented Israel's anticipated restoration: *In days to come Jacob will take root, Israel will bud and blossom and fill all the world with fruit* (Isaiah 27.6). Psalm 80 contains all three movements of exodus, exile, and renewal: *You transplanted a vine from Egypt; you drove out the nations and planted it. You cleared the ground for it, and it took root and filled the land. . . . Your vine is cut down, it is burned with fire; at your rebuke your people perish. . . . Restore us, LORD God Almighty; make your face shine on us, that we may be saved* (80.8-9, 16, 19). By uttering the words, "I am the vine. You are the branches" (John 15.5), Jesus unmistakably presents himself and his crew as the restored remnant of God's people.

Fifth, another popular prophetic image portrays restored Israel at a banquet feasting with God in a world made new. For instance, check out Isaiah 25.6-9:

> *On this mountain the LORD Almighty will prepare a feast of rich food for all peoples, a banquet of aged wine — the best of meats and the finest of wines. On this mountain he will destroy the shroud that enfolds all peoples, the sheet that covers all nations; he will swallow up death forever. The Sovereign LORD will wipe away the tears from all faces; he will remove his people's disgrace from all the earth. The LORD has spoken. In that day they will say, "Surely this is our God; we trusted in him, and he saved us. This is the LORD, we trusted in him; let us rejoice and be glad in his salvation."*

Jesus speaks of such a banquet in various ways, always in relation to God's kingdom and his own central role in the festivities (Matthew 8.11; Luke 13.28-29; 14.15-23; 22.29-30).

Sixth, Jesus' healings bore a social dimension we haven't yet mentioned. Sick people were considered "unclean" and therefore disqualified from full participation in the life and worship of Israel. This was especially true of those with skin diseases such as leprosy, as we read in Leviticus 13-14. Here is a representative sampling (Leviticus 13.9-11, 45-46):

> *When anyone has a defiling skin disease, they must be brought to the priest. The priest is to examine them, and if there is a white swelling in the skin that has turned the hair white and if there is raw flesh in the swelling, it is a chronic skin disease and the priest shall pronounce them unclean. He is not to isolate them, because they are already unclean.*

> *Anyone with such a defiling disease must wear torn clothes, let their hair be unkempt, cover the lower part of their face and cry out, 'Unclean! Unclean!' As long as they have the disease they remain unclean. They must live alone; they must live outside the camp.*

As Leviticus prescribes, those with such diseases had to undergo laborious ritual cleansing practices, and their cleanness had to be verified by priests before they were admitted back into the community of faith. Until then they remained outcasts. With this background in mind take a look at this story recorded in Matthew 8.1-4, Mark 1.40-45, and Luke 5.12-14:

> *When Jesus came down from the mountainside, large crowds followed him. A man with leprosy came and knelt before him and said, "Lord, if you are willing, you can make me clean."*
>
> *Jesus reached out his hand and touched the man. "I am willing," he said. "Be clean!" Immediately he was cleansed of his leprosy. Then Jesus said to him, "See that you don't tell anyone. But go, show yourself to the priest and offer the gift Moses commanded, as a testimony to them."*

Notice first that Jesus *touched the man*, which technically should have rendered Jesus unclean like the leper. But the opposite happened. Instead of the leper's uncleanness transferring to Jesus, Jesus' wholeness transferred to the leper. In addition to being healed, he was now clean as well. Jesus doesn't stop there, however, but instructs the man to undergo the prescribed purification rituals with the priests. Jesus' healing touch restores this man as a faithful member of God's family.

In all these ways (and a few more we haven't mentioned) we see that Jesus' kingdom-bringing mission is linked to the rehabilitation of God's people. Jesus' goals were communal through and through. Jesus sought the restoration of Israel as God's faithful family, the community in which God's kingdom would find its necessary home.

But "restore" alone insufficiently describes what Jesus did for his people. For them to embody God's kingdom, much more would have to happen than "returning to an earlier state of health or soundness" (which is the definition of "restore"). Jesus didn't aim to bring God's people *back* from a condition of exile to a state previously lost, but rather he sought to usher her forward to a place she had not yet been. Jesus' reforms were preparation for the good new day dawning in him.

REFORMING GOD'S KINGDOM COMMUNITY

All cultures have symbols that define who they are, where they've come from, what's important to them, and what they're trying to do. These symbols include actual objects such as the American flag or the Constitution, places like the White House or presidential monuments or Ellis Island, institutions such as family and capitalism and the Supreme Court, ideals like freedom and justice, traditions like baseball and barbecuing, and festivals such as Memorial Day and the Fourth of July. These artifacts, values, and practices define us as Americans, for example, and anyone seeking to reform American culture typically positions themselves in relation to one or more of these powerful symbols.

Jesus challenged virtually every cultural symbol that defined Israel as God's special people. (No wonder he got into so much trouble!) Among the primary symbols of Jewish identity were—and in many cases still are—the following:

(1) The Temple in Jerusalem. Here the presence of God dwelt on earth, here sacrifices were offered and forgiveness secured, and from here Israel's kings rightfully ruled the world. The Temple powerfully testified to Israel's place in the hierarchy of creation.

(2) Family. When you believe that you alone are God's chosen race, you tend to hold family in high regard, which is exactly what we see at every stage in Israel's history. To cite one example, consider how seriously they looked down upon marrying non-Israelites (Exodus 34.15; Deuteronomy 7.1-4; 1 Kings 11.1-10; Ezra 10.1-5; Nehemiah 13.23-30).

(3) Festivals. Thousands of ordinary Jewish folks flooded Jerusalem at least three times a year to celebrate three main festivals: Passover, commemorating Israel's exodus from Egypt. Pentecost (or the Feast of Weeks), celebrating when God gave Israel the Law (Torah). And the Feast of Tabernacles, recalling Israel's wanderings through the desert en route to the Promised Land. In addition to these three major festivals, most Jews also celebrated Hanukkah (also called the Festival of Lights or Feast of Dedication), which commemorated the Temple's rededication after the Maccabean brothers secured independence for Israel in 164 BC, and Purim, which

remembered God's protection of Israel from Persian plots during the time of Esther. Much like American holidays such as Thanksgiving or Independence Day, all of these festivals told Israel's story in a way that continued to shape her identity.

(4) Torah. Not only was the Law considered just, right, good, and even perfect (Nehemiah 9.13; Psalm 19.7), it also set Israel apart as God's uniquely chosen ones: *"Now if you obey me fully and keep my covenant, then out of all nations you will be my treasured possession. Although the whole earth is mine, you will be for me a kingdom of priests and a holy nation"* (Exodus 19.5-6; see also Deuteronomy 4.8). Down to our own day, the care and seriousness with which the sacred scrolls are handled testify to the preeminent value placed on the Torah.

(5) Ritual Purity. Remember how defiling skin diseases disqualified afflicted people from being full members of God's people? This is one of many examples of the Jews' high regard for ritual cleanness, which was a prerequisite for drawing near to God. Separation from anything unholy was considered by many (especially the Pharisees) to be a requirement before obtaining God's forgiveness, blessing, and deliverance.

Jesus messed with every item on this list.

First, he reserved some of harshest words, which we'll study a bit more in the next chapter, for the Temple in Jerusalem. In addition to his famous demonstration there (when he turned over the tables and accused the money-changers of turning God's holy house into a "den of robbers"), Jesus once predicted the Temple's complete destruction: *Jesus left the temple and was walking away when his disciples came up to him to call his attention to its buildings. "Do you see all these things?" he asked. "Truly I tell you, not one stone here will be left on another; every one will be thrown down"* (Matthew 24.1-2). He knew that the Temple was no longer necessary because *"something greater than the temple is here"* (Matthew 12.6; see also John 2.19-22). In a way no one could have understood without the benefit of hindsight, Jesus himself was the place where God's presence dwelt on earth, where sins were atoned for and forgiveness secured, and from which God ruled all creation.

Second, Jesus similarly redefined the idea of family and ethnic identity. Once, when Jesus was informed that his mother and brothers wanted a word with him outside (because they feared he was out of his mind), notice how he responded: *"Who are my mother and my brothers?" he asked. Then he looked at those seated in a circle around him and said, "Here are my mother and my brothers! Whoever does God's will is my brother and sister and mother"* (Mark 3.20-21, 31-35). Good Jewish boys just don't say such things! But Jesus did. Not only did he fearlessly divide his own family based on whether they followed him, he unashamedly demanded the same of others: *"If anyone comes to me and does not hate father and mother, wife and children, brothers and sisters – yes, even their own life – such a person cannot be my disciple"* (Luke 14.26; see also Matthew 10.34-39). No longer were men and women defined as God's people because they had the blood of Abraham and Moses in their veins. God's people were now defined as those who gave up everything for the sake of following Jesus.

Third, of all the Gospels, John in particular shows Jesus gaining a hearing and even stirring up controversy – whether intentionally or by accident it is difficult to say! – at both major and minor Jewish festivals: Tabernacles (7.1-52), Hanukkah/Dedication (10.22-42), and above all Passover (2.23; 4.45; 6.1-15; 11.55ff). In all four Gospels, Jesus interprets his upcoming death as a fulfillment of the hopes and aspirations expressed in the Passover (which we'll study more about in chapter six).

Fourth, central to Jesus' reforming agenda was his relationship to the Jewish Law (what we call the Old Testament). Unlike his attitude toward the Temple, Jesus held the Law in high regard. He didn't come to destroy or even replace it, but to fulfill it: *"Do not think that I have come to abolish the Law or the Prophets; I have not come to abolish them but to fulfill them. For truly I tell you, until heaven and earth disappear, not the smallest letter, not the least stroke of a pen, will by any means disappear from the Law until everything is accomplished"* (Matthew 5.17-18).

However, we mustn't let his kind words lead us to underplay how much his "fulfillment" redefined obedience to God. Notice the context in which Jesus says these words in Matthew 5. The rest of the chapter shows Jesus either intensifying or reversing Israel's sacred commands using the formula, "You've heard it said... but I say unto you." Don't miss what's happening here: Jesus places his own words ("but I say unto you") in some sense above God's ancient commands in the Law ("You've heard it said")! He's not saying the Law is bad, but its time is up because the one to whom it pointed has arrived. Faithfulness to the One True God was no longer measured by how well your life lined up to the Law revealed to Moses, but by how closely you aligned yourself with Jesus.

Finally, as we discovered when we talked about Jesus touching and healing a leper, Jesus pulled the rug out from under the central idea behind ritual purity—that human brokenness contaminates the faithful. On the contrary, Jesus' compassion "contaminated" sick folks with health and life and love. The net effect of Israel's commitment to ritual purity was that certain people became untouchables, outcasts, and misfits. This included those who were sick or deformed simply by bad luck, as well as those whose willful sin (such as prostitution or tax collecting) put them on the outside looking in. Jesus refused to play by the rules of this game.

Consider just one example: In John 4, Jesus starts a conversation with the last person he should talk to. First, she was a woman, which meant she was out of bounds for a Jewish man like Jesus. Second, she was a Samaritan. As John himself points out, Jews didn't associate with Samaritans because they were regarded as unclean half-breeds (John 4.9; see 2 Kings 17.24-41). Third, as we say today, she had a past. Whether she was intentionally promiscuous or often taken advantage of, she had been married five times and was now living with a man who was not her husband. She likely came to the well at midday—despite the miserable heat!—so she wouldn't run into the other ladies drawing water. They knew all her not-so-secrets and may have been less than compassionate about them. In spite of all these reasons, however, Jesus talked to her. What's more, she became his primary witness in her hometown, with the result that many Samaritans believed in Jesus as *the Savior of the world* (4.1-42).

Jesus did this kind of thing all the time. Jesus accepted adoration from a prostitute, rescued a woman caught—or framed—in adultery, and dined with tax collectors and sinners

(Luke 7.36-50; John 7.53-8.11; Matthew 9.9-13; see also Luke 14.15-24). His meals stand out in this regard because, for a movement leader like Jesus, to eat with someone basically meant he accepted them as part of his group. When Jesus ate with people, he registered them as part of the renewed people of God. This last feature of Jesus' restoration and reformation project deserves much more space than we can give it here. It is, in fact, one of the most distinguishable traits of Jesus' movement: all the wrong people were invited. Everyone was welcome.

In all these ways (and no doubt many more!), Jesus reformed God's family by redefining it around himself. He is the kingdom community's true north, its focal point, its measuring stick. He is its one and only center.

THE CHALLENGE OF JESUS TODAY

Jesus isn't asking for a minor role in the stories we're already writing. He wants to re-story our lives as a whole. Jesus came here to establish God's reign by restoring and reforming God's family, and he invites us to accept the story of God's kingdom community as our own. He seeks nothing less than a thorough transformation — of our identities and dreams, our agendas and priorities, our hopes and imaginations. Nonetheless we need a few insights into what difference this makes right now.

For starters, as followers of Jesus, whatever was central to Jesus' life should also be central to our lives. Put simply, God's kingdom matters for us, and we must let it become one of the primary lenses through which we view our lives. God's kingdom ought to pervade our thoughts, our lives, our prayers. The story of God's kingdom is the story into which we've been invited, even if we're still discovering what role to play. So our first challenge is to define our lives in relation to God's kingdom, to become the kind of people for whom God's kingdom matters. Or as Jesus put it, to *seek first the kingdom of God.*

Our second challenge is to avoid the common mistake of redefining God's kingdom to fit what we already care about. The "kingdom of God" is not an empty container we can fill with whatever we think is right, important, or good. We don't get to create our own goals, mission, to-do list, program, or ethic and then stamp "Christian" on it as if this label alone ensures that God is pleased, that God willingly accepts this as part of his reign. God's reign is Jesus, or more accurately, God's reign always looks like Jesus. The kingdom always looks like Jesus because in Jesus the kingdom came. If you want to see the realm over which God rules as king, where his name is properly honored and his will promptly done, look first and finally at Jesus.

Thirdly, Jesus challenges our assumption that life is about me. Of course we recognize the destructive power of "selfishness," but I'm talking about something deeper than that. We tend to operate as if other people are secondary to *my* journey or goals or agenda, whether they pertain to a career, having fun, or knowing God. But as a friend of mine often says, "The Christian life is not an individual pursuit of perfection. It's a shared journey as we together walk the way of Jesus." Jesus himself would most definitely agree. If you consider yourself spiritual but think your spirituality is merely a personal relationship with God, you need to reconsider. Jesus came not to restore individuals but the *family* of God, and only together can we become what he has made us.

Our fourth challenge is for us, the church, to understand our identity as the fulfillment and continuation of the Old Testament community of faith (Galatians 3.29; 6.13-16; Ephesians 2.11-22; also compare 1 Peter 2.9-10 with Exodus 19.5-6 and Hosea 1.2-11). *Our* God is the God of Abraham, Isaac, Jacob, Moses, David, Esther, Isaiah, and the rest. This story matters because it is our story. We are the restored and renewed family of God, the alternative community called to embody a different kind of kingdom. We are the church. Moreover, to truly be the church— the folks through whom God has chosen to continue his redemptive mission—we remain singularly centered on Jesus. Other traditions, values, practices, and commitments have their place, but they must never compete with our primary allegiance to Jesus.

Fifth and finally, welcoming all the "wrong people" into the family is vital for our unique witness in the world. If we as a church aren't filled with untouchables, outcasts, and misfits, we're centering ourselves on something other than Jesus. Everyone is welcome in the church—no matter who you are, what you've done, or what you're doing—and together all are called to follow Jesus.

We'll flesh out more of what all this looks like in chapter five, but first we have to examine the flip side of all this good news. Let's take a look at Jesus' message of judgment.

Four

WHAT MADE JESUS ANGRY?

Of all the misperceptions of Jesus in our world, few are more annoying than the idea that Jesus was and is vanilla. I will often encourage folks interested in Jesus to read through one of the Gospels and note the following: What about Jesus do you find admirable? What about Jesus do you not like? What about Jesus do you find surprising? So far everyone I've taken through this exercise has included in the third category something about Jesus not being as *nice* as they expected. Apparently they either never knew or forgot that Jesus got angry on multiple occasions (Mark 1.41; 3.5), created quite a destructive ruckus in the Temple (John 2.13-17), called one of his closest friends Satan (Matthew 16.23), mocked a Roman politician by referring to him as a she-fox (by which he meant cowardly, not attractive; Luke 13.31-33), killed a herd of 2000 pigs without compensating the owners (Mark 5.11-13), and cursed an innocent fig tree in order to make a point about faith (Mark 11.12-14, 20-21). Jesus adeptly and creatively name-called with the best of them. To "Satan" and "she-fox" we can add the following: blind guides, whitewashed tombs, snakes, brood of vipers, sons of the devil, liar, dog (to a woman no less!), ignorant, dull, and faithless (see, in order, Matthew 23.16, 27, 33; John 8.44, 55; Mark 7.26-27; 12.24; Matthew 15.16; Luke 9.41).

In spite of such evidence, images live on in some quarters of Jesus as little more than a next-door-neighborish nice guy; a polite, churchy type; or an enlightened, inclusive, and above all "spiritual" guru who loves lattes, self-help books, and Buddhists.

Now don't get me wrong. Jesus doesn't appear in the Gospels as arbitrarily surly or bullish either. Characterizations of Jesus as an MMA-like tough guy who woos would-be followers with his ability to beat people up are hardly easier to stomach.

But for our purposes the point is not whether he was mean or nice, playful or pokerfaced, even-tempered or moody. The point is that central to Jesus' message was a word of judgment.

In the last chapter we began unpacking the ministry of Jesus. In order to better grasp who Jesus is, we started digging into what he actually did and how his actions work and fit together. We learned that Jesus' all-encompassing goal was to establish or inaugurate God's kingdom, and that this involved restoring and reforming God's people. Now let's add a third item to our list of Jesus' aims: to warn of God's impending judgment. Jesus came to usher in the great "day of the Lord" Israel had anticipated for so long. And like so many prophets before him, Jesus brought an unwelcome word of judgment to those who expected nothing but good news. This "day" would present a moment of crisis for Israel, one that would forever alter the landscape not only of the Jewish homeland, but also of the identity of the people of God. In this chapter we'll examine both the manner of God's judgment as well as the reasons for it. And we'll walk away with a pretty solid answer to this chapter's question: *What Made Jesus Angry?*

WARNING OF GOD'S JUDGMENT

Let's start with a few representative samples of judgment-talk from Jesus from Matthew 11.20-24 and 23.33-36, Luke 13.1-5, and John 8.42-47:

> *Then Jesus began to denounce the towns in which most of his miracles had been performed, because they did not repent. "Woe to you, Chorazin! Woe to you, Bethsaida! For if the miracles that were performed in you had been performed in Tyre and Sidon, they would have repented long ago in sackcloth and ashes. But I tell you, it will be more bearable for Tyre and Sidon on the day of judgment than for you. And you, Capernaum, will you be lifted to the heavens? No, you will go down to Hades. For if the miracles that were performed in you had been*

performed in Sodom, it would have remained to this day. But I tell you that it will be more bearable for Sodom on the day of judgment than for you."

"You snakes! You brood of vipers! How will you escape being condemned to hell? Therefore I am sending you prophets and sages and teachers. Some of them you will kill and crucify; others you will flog in your synagogues and pursue from town to town. And so upon you will come all the righteous blood that has been shed on earth, from the blood of righteous Abel to the blood of Zechariah son of Berekiah, whom you murdered between the temple and the altar. Truly I tell you, all this will come on this generation."

Now there were some present at that time who told Jesus about the Galileans whose blood Pilate had mixed with their sacrifices. Jesus answered, "Do you think that these Galileans were worse sinners than all the other Galileans because they suffered this way? I tell you, no! But unless you repent, you too will all perish. Or those eighteen who died when the tower in Siloam fell on them – do you think they were more guilty than all the others living in Jerusalem? I tell you, no! But unless you repent, you too will all perish."

Jesus said to them, "If God were your Father, you would love me, for I have come here from God. I have not come on my own; God sent me. Why is my language not clear to you? Because you are unable to hear what I say. You belong to your father, the devil, and you want to carry out your father's desires. He was a murderer from the beginning, not holding to the truth, for there is no truth in him. When he lies, he speaks his native language, for he is a liar and the father of lies. Yet because I tell the truth, you do not believe me! Can any of you prove me guilty of sin? If I am telling the truth, why don't you believe me? Whoever belongs to God hears what God says. The reason you do not hear is that you do not belong to God."

Told you he wasn't always nice.

Using somewhat colorful language, here we see Jesus in different ways warning people that they were on the wrong side of God's coming judgment. This raises numerous questions, two of which we'll answer presently: *Why was God's judgment coming?* and *What would God's judgment look like?*

THE "WHY" OF GOD'S JUDGMENT

Why would God judge his people? Why would God position himself against them? What had they done wrong?

The answer has two basic dimensions, which I can best explain using an analogy of a baseball team. Baseball teams have one overriding purpose: to win baseball games. But this baseball team stinks. They lose many more games than they win. After some time and quite a few trades, management decides the time has come to fire the old coach and bring in a new one. The new coach arrives at spring training looking to change the team's losing ways. Both he and the players know that in the process some of them will be cut from the team. Some simply aren't skilled enough. Others have gotten too used to losing to be part of the culture change that is necessary to start winning. Still others don't play baseball in a way that fits with the new coach's schemes or plans or style. So they eventually find themselves on the outside looking in. They were cut because of (1) what they had done (or not done) in the past — whatever contributed to all those losses — and (2) what they were unwilling to do in the present, that is, to play in a way that lined up with the coach's winning strategy.

The team is God's people and the incoming coach is Jesus. The first dimension had to do with what they had done (or not done) in the past. In various ways which we'll examine below, Israel had failed to fulfill her task as the vessel through which God's blessing would reach out and grab hold of the rest of us. Though called to be the light of the world — to be set apart, holy, different — Israel had once again become just another kingdom of the world. As such, she had hindered God from revealing a true alternative to the arrogant, death-dealing, manipulative, self-deluded kingdoms of the world. And the second dimension concerned the new thing God was doing in Jesus. In him, God was unveiling his "winning strategy," so to speak. He was finally and fully revealing his will for his people and the world at large. But most folks didn't want to play the game Jesus' way. As Jesus

72

put it, they would see every stone in Jerusalem overturned because they *did not recognize the time of God's coming* (Luke 19.44).

In a general sense, that is "why" God was going to judge them. Let's get more specific by unpacking the image below:

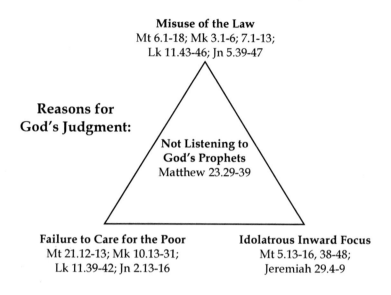

Misuse of the Law
Mt 6.1-18; Mk 3.1-6; 7.1-13;
Lk 11.43-46; Jn 5.39-47

Reasons for God's Judgment:

Not Listening to God's Prophets
Matthew 23.29-39

Failure to Care for the Poor
Mt 21.12-13; Mk 10.13-31;
Lk 11.39-42; Jn 2.13-16

Idolatrous Inward Focus
Mt 5.13-16, 38-48;
Jeremiah 29.4-9

We begin at the top with the subject of most of Jesus' fights with the Jewish religious leaders: how to faithfully obey God's Law. The people who made Jesus angry turned a gift designed to bring liberation into a curse feeding arrogance and oppression. First of all, they used the Law as a tool to make themselves look good and win respect among their peers (Matthew 6.1-18; Luke 11.43). Their second offense against the Law was simple hypocrisy: They required others to do what they weren't willing to do themselves. They loaded people with burdens they weren't willing to help carry. Jesus confronted them on this very point: *"And you experts in the law, woe to you, because you load people down with burdens they can hardly carry, and you yourselves will not lift one finger to help them"* (Luke 11.46).

Certain groups within Judaism also followed a body of oral traditions designed to safeguard the Law. The idea was to run as far from disobedience as possible. So since the Law said don't work on the Sabbath without spelling out exactly what "work" entailed, they established clearer parameters regarding things like how far you can walk, what does and doesn't constitute cooking (and therefore working), and so on. The unfortunate result was that in some cases their "safeguards" caused them to completely miss the Law's underlying spirit.

Let's talk more about the Sabbath, for instance. The idea of Sabbath was that for one day out of seven, everyone—including slaves and even the land itself—got a break. God gave the Sabbath for people's sake—so they could rest from all their labor, relax, and heal up for another week of hard work. Devout Jews took the Sabbath very seriously, in large part because God had promised a tight link between keeping the Sabbath and Israel's restoration (Nehemiah 13.16-18; Isaiah 58.13-14; Jeremiah 17.19-27; also Exodus 31.12-17). But in their effort to safeguard it, they outlawed *healing* on the Sabbath, because healing was considered work. This background helps us understand stories like the one in Mark 3.1-6 (see also John 5.1-18):

> *Another time Jesus went into the synagogue, and a man with a shriveled hand was there. Some of them were looking for a reason to accuse Jesus, so they watched him closely to see if he would heal him on the Sabbath. Jesus said to the man with the shriveled hand, "Stand up in front of everyone."*
>
> *Then Jesus asked them, "Which is lawful on the Sabbath: to do good or to do evil, to save life or to kill?" But they remained silent.*
>
> *He looked around at them in anger and, deeply distressed at their stubborn hearts, said to the man, "Stretch out your hand." He stretched it out, and his hand was completely restored. Then the Pharisees went out and began to plot with the Herodians how they might kill Jesus.*

In this case, their religious traditions competed with the Law's original spirit. Sometimes their traditions led to flat-out disobedience. A few chapters later in Mark's Gospel, we again find Jesus fighting with the Pharisees and teachers of the Law about obedience to God. Jesus' disciples were eating without the proper ceremonial hand washings. When some Pharisees and teachers of the law confronted Jesus on this point, he turned the tables on them: *"You have let go of the commands of God and are holding on to human traditions"* (Mark 7.8). He then went after one of their traditions called Corban—which means "devoted to God"—whereby living Jewish folks dedicated their money and resources to the Temple after their death. This became a problem when people started labeling their estates "Corban" so they didn't have to use it to take care of their own moms and dads! They broke the fifth commandment for the sake of their tradition, which Jesus pointed out: *"Thus you nullify the word of God by your tradition that you have handed down. And you do many things like that"* (Mark 7.13; see 7.1-23 for the whole story).

These misuses of the Law bleed into the second corner of our triangle: not caring for the poor. We saw last chapter how much of first century Judaism manifested a lack of concern for marginalized folks such as the sick and diseased. Along similar lines, Jesus was *indignant* with his disciples when they tried to keep little kids from bothering him (Mark 10.13-16). Jesus had an affinity for anything small, vulnerable, or typically forgotten. This affinity included the economically poor of course, as we see from the way Jesus castigated Jewish leaders in Luke 11.39-42:

> *Then the Lord said to him, "Now then, you Pharisees clean the outside of the cup and dish, but inside you are full of greed and wickedness. You foolish people! Did not the one who made the outside make the inside also? But now as for what is inside you—be generous to the poor, and everything will be clean for you. Woe to you Pharisees, because you give God a tenth of your mint, rue and all other kinds of garden herbs, but you neglect justice and the love of God. You should have practiced the latter without leaving the former undone.*

Notice how Jesus defines inward godliness as giving to the poor. Though they scrupulously kept less important aspects of God's Law, this they lacked. They majored in the minors, or as Jesus put it, strained a gnat but swallowed a camel (Matthew 23.23-24).

This illuminates Jesus' demonstration in the Temple. He began his final week by riding into Jerusalem like a king, after which he *entered the temple courts and drove out all who were buying and selling there. He overturned the tables of the money changers and the benches of those selling doves. "It is written," he said to them, "'My house will be called a house of prayer,' but you are making it 'a den of robbers'"* (Matthew 21.12-13; see also Mark 11.15-19; Luke 19.45-48; John 2.13-16). For our immediate purposes, notice that Jesus particularly targeted those who sold *doves* for sacrificing to God, which as we noted earlier was what poor folks like Jesus' parents offered when they couldn't afford the required lamb (Leviticus 5.7; 12.8; Luke 2.22-24). Remembering what we learned in chapter two about how Temple authorities made their money, we might expect such a reaction from Jesus. (See also Mark 10.17-31; Luke 1.53; 6.24; 12.13-21; 16.19-31.) Put simply, those who profited off the poor made Jesus angry.

Rounding out our triangle, in these and other ways Israel had failed in her one all-encompassing task. Remember God's call to Abraham, which stands before and behind everything about God's chosen people. In Isaiah's words, Israel would be *a light for the Gentiles, that salvation may reach to the ends of the earth* (49.6; see also Isaiah 2.2-4; 11.9-10; 42.1-6; Micah 4.1-4). The problem as Jesus saw it was that Israel had kept this light to herself. She was like a lamp oddly placed under a bowl so that the rest of the house remained in darkness. She was salt that had lost its saltiness, no longer serving any purpose (Matthew 5.13-16; Luke 8.16). Israel had made an idol of herself—of her special identity as God's chosen race—and was bent on destroying whatever blocked her gain and glory. Long ago, Jeremiah had counseled God's people to replace their vengeful spirit with a desire to bless even the hated cities of their captors (Jeremiah 29.4-9):

> *This is what the LORD Almighty, the God of Israel, says to all those I carried into exile from Jerusalem to Babylon: "Build houses and settle down; plant gardens and eat what they produce. Marry and have sons and daughters; find wives for your sons and give your daughters in marriage, so that they too may have sons and daughters. Increase in number there; do not decrease. Also, seek the peace and prosperity of the city to which I have carried you into exile. Pray to the LORD for it, because if it prospers, you too will prosper." Yes, this is what the LORD Almighty, the God of Israel, says: "Do not let the prophets and diviners among you deceive you. Do not listen to the dreams you encourage them to have. They are prophesying lies to you in my name. I have not sent them," declares the LORD.*

Prophetic words such as these stand behind Jesus' call for his people to cease plotting revolt and start loving their enemies as they loved themselves (Matthew 5.38-48).

Denouncing Israel's injustice, hypocrisy, and idolatrous inward focus was hardly a new thing. Prophets had been making a living (or a dying, as it were) condemning these things for centuries. For this, too, Israel merited God's wrath. His people had rejected the very servants He had sent to get their attention. The irony, according to Jesus, was that those who in his own day celebrated the memory of such prophets — and even decorated their tombs out of respect — repeated the sins of the people who put them to death! For this reason Jerusalem's house — that is, the Temple — would be "left to them desolate" (Matthew 23.29-39).

There's one more thing we mustn't forget. God's judgment was coming not simply because people did or didn't *do* certain things right. God's judgment was coming because his people rejected Jesus. Remember our baseball analogy? The coach didn't just cut players who weren't good enough, he released those who refused to align with where he was taking the team. Let's talk through one modification to our triangle and then we'll move on.

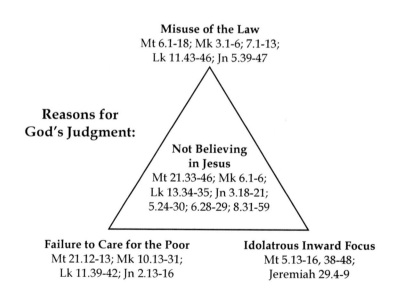

Misuse of the Law
Mt 6.1-18; Mk 3.1-6; 7.1-13;
Lk 11.43-46; Jn 5.39-47

**Reasons for
God's Judgment:**

**Not Believing
in Jesus**
Mt 21.33-46; Mk 6.1-6;
Lk 13.34-35; Jn 3.18-21;
5.24-30; 6.28-29; 8.31-59

Failure to Care for the Poor
Mt 21.12-13; Mk 10.13-31;
Lk 11.39-42; Jn 2.13-16

Idolatrous Inward Focus
Mt 5.13-16, 38-48;
Jeremiah 29.4-9

God didn't reject his people simply for not being good enough. God rejected his people for rejecting Jesus. Or, to say it another way, God accepted the rejection of those who rejected Jesus. In the life of this one man Jesus of Nazareth, God came to reveal the way of salvation and welcome everyone to accept a place within his saving reign. Those who didn't enter faced the repercussions of remaining outside, where God's wrath is revealed — which is to say, where God turns people over to the consequences of their own destructive ways of life. In the words of Jesus from Luke 19.42-44:

> As he approached Jerusalem and saw the city, he wept over it and said, "If you, even you, had only known on this day what would bring you peace — but now it is hidden from your eyes. The days will come upon you when your enemies will build an embankment against you and encircle you and hem you in on every side. They will dash you to the ground, you and the children within your walls. They will not leave one stone on another, because you did not recognize the time of God's coming to you."

They refused to know what — or who — would bring them peace, so they will see their rejection of God's purposes through to the end. What specifically was Jesus talking about? What form would God's judgment take in his own day? This brings us to our second question.

THE "HOW" OF GOD'S JUDGMENT

How exactly would this judgment come about? If you look back to Jesus' judgments quoted earlier in this chapter, Jesus is clearly talking about something that will happen to his own generation of Jews (see also Mark 13.30 in context). But what would it look like? How would it happen?

The answer, believe it or not, is Rome. Like he had so often in the past with Assyria, Babylon, and the like, God planned to use Israel's enemies to enforce judgment on His own people. Consider again Jesus' words in Luke 13.3:

Now there were some present at that time who told Jesus about the Galileans whose blood Pilate had mixed with their sacrifices. Jesus answered, "Do you think that these Galileans were worse sinners than all the other Galileans because they suffered this way? I tell you, no! But unless you repent, you too will all perish.

When Jesus says *"Unless you repent, you too will all perish,"* what is he talking about? Here some people tell Jesus about a time when Pilate, the Roman governor overseeing Judea, put to death a bunch of Jewish freedom fighters inside the sanctuary itself. Jesus warns that unless they repent, they'll meet a similar fate.

Another example can be found in Luke 19.42-44, which we quoted in the last section.

As he approached Jerusalem and saw the city, he wept over it and said, "If you, even you, had only known on this day what would bring you peace – but now it is hidden from your eyes. The days will come upon you when your enemies will build an embankment against you and encircle you and hem you in on every side. They will dash you to the ground, you and the children within your walls. They will not leave one stone on another, because you did not recognize the time of God's coming to you."

Everyone at the time knew that by "enemies" Jesus meant Roman soldiers, and in fact Jesus' words here proved true within a generation. In 66 AD, Jewish rebels took control of the Temple and from there staged a major rebellion against Rome. By the end of the war four years later, the Temple was destroyed, Rome's preeminence was restored, and the Jews were once again defeated. All this happened just as Jesus predicted (see also Matthew 24; Mark 13; Luke 21). These are the events Jesus also spoke of in places like Luke 17.31-36 and 21.20-23:

"In that day no one who is on the housetop, with possessions inside, should go down to get them. Likewise, no one in the field should go back for anything. Remember Lot's wife! Whoever tries to keep their life will lose it, and whoever loses their life will preserve it. I tell you, on that night two people will be in

one bed; one will be taken and the other left. Two women will be grinding grain together; one will be taken and the other left."

"When you see Jerusalem being surrounded by armies, you will know that its desolation is near. Then let those who are in Judea flee to the mountains, let those in the city get out, and let those in the country not enter the city. For this is the time of punishment in fulfillment of all that has been written. How dreadful it will be in those days for pregnant women and nursing mothers! There will be great distress in the land and wrath against this people. They will fall by the sword and will be taken as prisoners to all the nations."

The former passage describes soldiers sweeping through the countryside to kill and pillage. And the latter accurately portrays the events that came to pass a few short decades later.

Jesus saw clearly that Israel's rejection of God's way of salvation, and in particular her refusal to view Rome as someone to bless rather than hate, would in the end lead to Rome doing what Rome always did: squash revolutions like only a powerful empire can. Taking it one step further, Jesus interpreted the coming destruction not as Rome getting the best of God, but of God using Rome as a tool to display his rejection of those who rejected Jesus.

GOD'S JUDGMENT THEN AND NOW

In chapter six we'll explore the "how" of God's judgment in relation to you and me. For now let me say this: Just as God surrendered Jerusalem to the consequences of Israel's sin, God will release us to the repercussions of our own rebellion. God's "wrath" works precisely in this way (see Romans 1.18-31).

While it may take some work to connect our lives with tragic but obscure events in the middle of the first century, the *reasons* for Jesus' message of judgment resonate all too well. The things that make Jesus angry haven't exactly gone away, and we hardly find them exclusively outside the doors of the church.

The misuse of religion—whether for puffing ourselves up, looking good without actually being good, or maintaining distance from "those people" — makes Jesus angry. Failing to care for the poor and vulnerable — whether physically, socially, politically, emotionally, or indeed economically — makes Jesus angry. Trying to keep God's blessing to ourselves — our race, our nation, our church, our denomination, our religion — makes Jesus angry. Refusing to listen to those God sends to warn us, strange and incomprehensible as they may seem, makes Jesus angry. In these ways we reject Jesus, and God will once again accept the rejection of those who reject Jesus.

Five

WHAT DID JESUS TEACH?

I know few people who don't think Jesus was, as they say, a "great moral teacher." Unfortunately, many consider him to be no more than this. Also unfortunately, I know about as many people who use their belief that Jesus was much more than a teacher in order to ignore Jesus' great moral teachings. In this chapter I hope to avoid both errors as we explore the question *What did Jesus teach?*

Someone once said, "God created us in his image and then we returned the favor," and this certainly rings true when it comes to Jesus and his teachings. We all like a Jesus who looks like us and teaches what we've already decided we want to do. Let's look at two examples: Deepak Chopra and Sam Bowers.

You may have heard of Deepak Chopra since he's one of Oprah's friends. Chopra is a doctor, speaker, and writer well versed in both Western medicine and Eastern spirituality. He's a spiritual-psychological guru of sorts. For the record, I have nothing at all against him personally. He seems warm, fairly intelligent, and genuinely caring. But he's very confused about who Jesus is, even though he's written multiple books about him. When he was asked "Who is/was Jesus?" this is what he said:

> In the eastern traditions there is the concept of avatars or bodhisattvas — enlightened beings. In Buddhism, the idea is that these enlightened beings are at the edge of what is called the dharmakaya and the sambhogakaya. The sambhogakaya is the realm of enlightened beings and the

dharmakaya is beyond that event horizon where there is the infinite intention of all that is, was, and will be. When beings reach this edge between the sambhogakaya and dharmakaya, they are at the door and have a choice to go beyond the event horizon and disappear from our realm or to come back and help others to where they are. In Hinduism, or the Vedantic tradition, they are called avatars, while in Buddhism they are called bodhisattvas because they have infinite compassion. As you know compassion is also an important aspect of Jesus. In many parts of India, depending on your vocabulary or semantics, Jesus is considered to be a bodhisattva, an avatar, or an enlightened being who has infinite compassion and wants to help others come out of their suffering. Jesus introduced the idea (which was very foreign to the older traditions of Judaism) of forgiveness, of love, of equality, of salvation rather than the Old Testament God that was like a dysfunctional parent.[1]

Notice how Chopra snatches elements from the actual teachings of Jesus and re-narrates them in a manner foreign to the actual story of Jesus. This isn't to say that Chopra is *entirely* wrong: Jesus does teach compassion, forgiveness, and love, and living by them will probably do more good than harm. But the real Jesus is so much more, as the rest of this book makes clear. In the end, to a world in need of a Savior and Lord, Jesus as a bodhisattva or an avatar just isn't enough. Chopra's Jesus, no doubt attractive in some respects, neither matches Scripture nor meets the deep needs of a world lost in corruption and bondage to sin.

Our second example, Sam Bowers, may very well break your heart. He was, on the one hand, a radically committed believer in orthodox Christianity. Listen to his words regarding Christ's resurrection: "There is one simple, and central, Empirical Fact, of manifested human history: That Empirical Fact, of course, is the Physical Resurrection of The Galilean.... The genuineness of Faith is in the Omnipotent Power of God to perform the Miracle." On the other hand, he was a key mid-20th century leader of the

---

[1] William Elliott, *A Place at the Table* (New York: Doubleday, 2003), 57.

white supremacist Ku Klux Klan. Concerned about the influx of blacks and communists, Bowers and his friends engaged in overt acts of violence against innocent people. What's worse, they did this in the name of Jesus. As Klan members gathered on June 7, 1964, armed with weapons in their hands and hatred in their hearts, the following prayer was offered before Bowers got up to prepare the troops for what they considered a veritable holy war:

> Oh God, our Heavenly guide, as finite creatures of time and as dependent creatures of Thine, we acknowledge Thee as our sovereign Lord. Permit freedom and the joys thereof to forever reign throughout our land. May we as klansmen forever have the courage of our convictions that we may always stand for Thee and for our great nation. May the sweet cup of brotherly fraternity ever be ours to enjoy and build within us that kindred spirit which will keep us unified and strong. Engender within us that wisdom kindred to honorable decisions and the Godly work. By the power of Thy infinite spirit and the energizing virtue therein, ever keep before us our oaths of secrecy and pledges of righteousness. Bless us now in this assembly that we may honor Thee in all things, we pray in the name of Christ, our blessed Savior. Amen.[2]

Not all who claim the name of Jesus look like Jesus. Sometimes, in fact, quite the opposite is tragically true.

Now obviously this is an extreme example but it illustrates a sin we all commit in one way or another: thinking Jesus taught whatever we think is important and right and good.

JESUS MEANT WHAT HE SAID

Though few of us will be tempted to mount horses and engage in racial violence in the name of Jesus, or to re-imagine Jesus within an Eastern religious framework, we all find ways to avoid obeying the actual teachings of Jesus.

---

[2] Alan Hirsch and Michael Frost, *ReJesus* (Peabody: Hendrickson, 2008), 1-2.

First, we sometimes divorce Jesus' teachings from everything else he did, as if he were no more than a giver of good advice. This mistake will ruin us, so let's not make it. So far we've unfolded three aspects of Jesus' mission: announcing and establishing God's kingdom, restoring and reforming God's family, and warning of God's judgment. To these three we now add a fourth: clarifying and revealing God's will. Both *clarify* and *reveal* are important for, as we will see, Jesus both built on what God had revealed before and completed God's revelation in new and sometimes surprising ways. But even the surprising parts don't stand alone. They form part of the broader goals Jesus came to accomplish.

Second and more commonly, we creatively set aside Jesus' teachings, which is a nice way of saying we either ignore them or act as if they weren't actually meant to be obeyed. Sometimes Christians have believed Jesus' teachings present an ethic for a world other than our own. Perhaps they were designed for a short-term movement awaiting the imminent end of the world. Maybe they only work in the future, fully consummated kingdom of God. Along with this, some folks teach that Jesus didn't mean for us to actually practice what he preached, but taught what he did so we'd recognize our need for grace. This seems obvious to them given how impossible it would be to actually live like Jesus suggests (er, commands). Unfortunately—or fortunately, depending on how you look at it—Jesus clearly thought that his teachings were not to be just admired, but also obeyed. Check out Matthew 7.24-27 and 28.18-20, and John 14.15, 21, 23:

> *"Therefore everyone who hears these words of mine **and puts them into practice** is like a wise man who built his house on the rock. The rain came down, the streams rose, and the winds blew and beat against that house; yet it did not fall, because it had its foundation on the rock. But everyone who hears these words of mine and does not put them into practice is like a foolish man who built his house on sand. The rain came down, the streams rose, and the winds blew and beat against that house, and it fell with a great crash."*
>
> *Then Jesus came to them and said, "All authority in heaven and on earth has been given to me. Therefore go and make*

*disciples of all nations, baptizing them in the name of the Father and of the Son and of the Holy Spirit, and **teaching them to obey everything I have commanded you.** And surely I am with you always, to the very end of the age."*

*"If you love me, **keep my commands.**"*

*"Whoever **has my commands and keeps them** is the one who loves me. The one who loves me will be loved by my Father, and I too will love them and show myself to them."*

*"Anyone who loves me **will obey my teaching.** My Father will love them, and we will come to them and make our home with them."*

Once again, Jesus clearly thought his teachings were to be obeyed. In fact he considered anything else a recipe for ruining your life—or at least losing your house to the sea.

All this begs the question: What are the teachings of Jesus? For the remainder of this chapter we'll answer this question in two forms: First, what exactly are we looking at when we examine Jesus' teachings? Second, what did Jesus in fact tell us to do? How has he told us to live?

WHAT *ARE* THE TEACHINGS OF JESUS?

How you read instructions depends on the kind of instructions you're reading. If you're reading a manual for how to build a dollhouse or a Lego set, for instance, you'll methodically follow one step after another, expecting in a reasonably short period of time to have completed your project. If, on the other hand, you're reading instructions on how to be married, you'll instinctively realize that (a) implementing these directives will take longer than building a dollhouse, and (b) you'll have to discern which aspects best fit your particular marriage and which do not. Similarly, we may commit all kinds of blunders if we learn what Jesus taught before examining what kind of instructions we're reading.

First, Jesus' teachings are a description of the life made possible by the presence of God's kingdom. They embody the way of life that is indigenous to the kind of kingdom Jesus came to establish. We must never forget that the most famous collection of Jesus' teachings—what we call the Sermon on the Mount in Matthew 5-7—follows hot on the heels of Jesus' initial declaration that God's kingdom had arrived (see Matthew 4.12-17). In this sermon we discover what life looks like in the kingdom of God.

Second, Jesus' teachings are a response to God's outrageous love. The God revealed in Jesus is a God who graciously sends rain on both good and evil; who knows what we need before we ask and gives it abundantly; whose eye remains fixed in love on sparrows, not to mention you and me; who joyfully and tenderly takes such an intense interest in us that even our hairs are numbered; who disregards his own honor to forgive and welcome home wayward children; who, as we will explore very soon, didn't even spare his own Son but suffered his rejection and death at the hands of his enemies—us—as a demonstration of his radical love (see, in order, Matthew 5.43-48; 6.8; 7.7-11; Luke 12.6-7; 15.11-31; Romans 5.8; 8.32; 1 John 4.9-10). There is no question here of earning God's favor by obeying Jesus. Such affection could obviously never be merited, and thankfully it doesn't have to be, because God has already offered it in mercy and grace.

Third, Jesus' teachings serve as a constitution for his first-century Messianic revolution. This is perhaps especially true of large blocks of teaching such as the Sermon on the Mount. Throughout this book we've been careful not to overlook the immediate context of Jesus' first century ministry, and here we must continue this good habit. Many of Jesus specific teachings on such topics as divorce and remarriage, reconciliation, and justice for the poor find their first proper home in this context. When we learn their meaning there, the light they shed on our own world only becomes brighter.

Fourth, by embodying a different kind of kingdom, Jesus' teachings offer a counter-cultural way of life and thus an implicit challenge to the Roman Empire (as well as any other form the world takes). Had Jesus mounted a frontal assault on Rome, his movement would have failed by becoming just like Rome in the most important sense. Like Israel reproducing "Egypt" in her own sinful ways, Jesus' movement would have become yet one more kingdom of the world. Because Jesus sought a deeper revolution than plain old revolt could obtain, he chose instead to challenge Rome's idolatrous pride and injustice by creating alternative communities right under her thumb. He outflanked her by revealing to the world a better way — the way of God's kingdom.

Fifth, like other aspects of Jesus' ministry — healings, exorcisms, and so on — his teachings are an anticipation of new creation. We've learned how ancient Jews typically divided history into two eras: "this age" and "the age to come." As much as possible while still within the old age, Jesus teachings portray the kind of life that fits the age to come. They provide a sign and foretaste of this new world. As a matter of fact, the common phrase "eternal life" literally refers to *the life of the age to come*. Obviously this age hasn't yet fully come, but we see its present manifestation in the kind of community Jesus' teachings form and sustain.

Sixth, Jesus' teachings comprise one dimension of his saving work. Sometimes people talk like Jesus dying for our sins competes with Jesus teaching us how to live. Thankfully, we don't have to choose between the two. Part of how Jesus actually saves us — that is, delivers us from sin and its effects — is by modeling and leading us in a life liberated from sin. This is why the book of Hebrews calls Jesus our pioneer or "trailblazer" (2.10; 12.1-3). He clears a path for us to hike, and by walking in his steps we follow him along the way of salvation (having first accepted God's undeserved love and forgiveness, of course).

Seventh, Jesus' teachings are a "way of the heart" that goes beyond simply following the rules.[3] As Jesus makes clear in Luke 6.43-45 and elsewhere, he isn't interested in replacing one list of rules with another. As Jesus' contemporaries illustrated all too well with the Sabbath, you can make a ridiculously long list, check off every item, and still miss the point entirely. Obedience from the heart progresses beyond merely following rules to

---

[3] It's important to note that obedience from the heart is not about focusing more on interior motive than actual behavior. Remember how Jesus defined obedience from the inside out: generosity to the poor (Luke 11.41), not hours of introspective meditation to determine if we really *want* to do the right thing.

becoming the kind of people who *naturally* live out Jesus' vision of life in God's kingdom. Obedience reaches our core. The habit of obedience builds into us a deep desire to do nothing else, even when it hurts. We obey in order to become people who more naturally obey (and more thoroughly enjoy it).

Eighth, we don't rely merely on our own moral strength for all this. (Thank God!) Jesus' teachings display the fruit being produced in us by God's Spirit. The Apostle Paul makes clear that the Holy Spirit actively transforms our character to look more like Jesus (Galatians 5.13-25; Romans 8.1-17, 28-29).

Ninth, Jesus' teachings reveal and define what it means to reflect God's image faithfully in a fallen world. Think back to the story of God creating the world, and in particular human beings to represent his loving reign. As soon as we screwed that up, God sought a community to bear his kingdom faithfully. He chose Israel, and Jesus came from within Israel precisely in order to fulfill this calling. When we look at Jesus, we see God's kingdom, which means for the first and only time we see someone perfectly imaging God according to creation's original design. Here we catch more than just a glimpse of the purpose for which we too were created.

Furthermore, tenth, Jesus' teachings reveal and define God's will for your life. I include this point for the many people who express confusion about what God wants from them. Our best answer, once we've explained God's limitless love and undeserved grace, would be to point one another to Jesus' teachings and say, "What God wants is for you to live like that. Here is God's will for your life and mine."

WHAT DID JESUS TEACH?

All this is fine and good—even beautiful—but you may be thinking, "Get to it already! *What* does Jesus tell us to actually do?" Thankfully, someone asked Jesus a very similar question. Here is the conversation:

> *One of the teachers of the law came and heard them debating. Noticing that Jesus had given them a good answer, he asked*

him, "Of all the commandments, which is the most important?"

"The most important one," answered Jesus, "is this: 'Hear, O Israel: The Lord our God, the Lord is one. Love the Lord your God with all your heart and with all your soul and with all your mind and with all your strength.' The second is this: 'Love your neighbor as yourself.' There is no commandment greater than these."

"Well said, teacher," the man replied. "You are right in saying that God is one and there is no other but him. To love him with all your heart, with all your understanding and with all your strength, and to love your neighbor as yourself is more important than all burnt offerings and sacrifices."

When Jesus saw that he had answered wisely, he said to him, "You are not far from the kingdom of God." And from then on no one dared ask him any more questions.

In answering this way, Jesus recalls an ancient prayer known as the *Shema* from Deuteronomy 6.4-8. Jesus likely prayed this prayer multiple times a day. While Jesus' teachings certainly contain some fresh details, he frames them within this very common bit of ancient Hebrew wisdom: Love God, love people. For the sake of clarity we'll divide the second command into two separate but interlocking aspects, and we'll work through the teachings of Jesus for the remainder of this chapter under three headings: love God, love one another, and love your enemies.

LOVE GOD

Appreciating the beauty of a rose is not difficult. Nor is it hard to marvel at the majesty of a mountain or the wonder of a true lover or friend. Good and beautiful things naturally call forth from us appreciation, adoration, awe, and love. God is beautiful and good. For the most part, the God revealed in Jesus is not difficult to love, at least not if you're seeing him truly and clearly. At times loving God involves an act of the will just as much as loving anyone or anything, but in a deeper sense love for God is the natural response to knowing God accurately and seeing him clearly. Loving God is, as we said above, a response to God's love for us.

Loving God begins with trusting that God is present with us, and that his presence is beneficent. Gracious and compassionate is the Lord, we can hear the psalmists sing, and in his nearness we find joy and life and peace. We love God, and therefore we trust—sometimes in spite of what we see or how we feel—that he is in every way worthy of our love. Moreover and importantly, loving God means trusting that God was and is active in and through Jesus (John 6.29; 14.1; Mark 4.40; 5.34-36; 6.6).

Loving God also means choosing God over any would-be competitors vying for our affection, loyalty, or allegiance. In Jesus' day as well as our own, money certainly headlines this list of challengers. Of course it isn't the actual metal or paper, but what it offers and represents that woos us: the ability to do what we want or purchase what we need, security in the face of life's countless dangers, control over at least a small corner of the universe. No doubt money's very real power in this world led Jesus to talk about it so much (e.g. Matthew 6.19-34; Mark 10.17-31; Luke 12.13-21). Worrying, profiteering, hoarding, and a host of other money-related offenses signify a lack of faith in—and thus love for—the God who loves and provides for our needs. In his words, *"No one can serve two masters. Either you will hate the one and love the other, or you will be devoted to the one and despise the other. You cannot serve both God and money"* (Matthew 6.24).

In Jesus' day, political power and the safety it promises also competed with God for the affection and confidence of God's people. Here as elsewhere Jesus builds on consistent themes from the preaching of Israel's prophets, who time and again warned against relying on political alliances rather than their great and powerful God (2 Chronicles 16.7-9; Isaiah 30.1-5; 31.1-3; Jeremiah 17.5-10). In an oft-misunderstood episode from the Gospels, Jesus was once asked whether to pay taxes to Caesar (Matthew 22.15-22). He requested to see one of his questioner's coins and asked whose *image* was on it. Here is our clue to the point Jesus is making. Since Caesar's image was on the coin, the coin must belong to Caesar: *"So give back to Caesar what is Caesar's, and to God what is God's"* (22.21). Jesus assumes that whoever's *image* adorns an object is that object's rightful owner. Since Caesar's image is on the coin, the coin must belong to him. Caesar's image isn't on *you*, however; on the contrary, *God's* image is on you, so give yourselves—your trust, your loyalty, your dependence, your affection, your faith, your love—to God. In every age we must vigilantly refuse to trust in political power in a way that competes with our love for and faith in God.

Finally, loving and trusting God also means obeying Him no matter what. As we heard from Jesus earlier, love for and obedience to God can never be torn apart (see John 14.15, 21, 23; 1 John 3.1-6). What's more, the obedience Jesus calls for may very well cost us everything (Luke 14.26, 33; Mark 8.34-36; Matthew 10.37-38):

> *"If anyone comes to me and does not hate father and mother, wife and children, brothers and sisters — yes, even their own life — such a person cannot be my disciple."*

> *"Those of you who do not give up everything you have cannot be my disciples."*

> *Then Jesus called the crowd to him along with his disciples and said: "Whoever wants to be my disciple must deny themselves and take up their cross and follow me. For whoever wants to save their life will lose it, but whoever loses their life for me and for the gospel will save it. What good is it for someone to gain the whole world, yet forfeit their soul?"*

> *"Anyone who loves their father or mother more than me is not worthy of me; anyone who loves their son or daughter more than me is not worthy of me. Whoever does not take up their cross and follow me is not worthy of me."*

Note especially Jesus' call to *take up your cross*. Everyone knew the cross was an instrument of torture and death—reserved particularly for low classes and those who challenged the supremacy of Rome. At the very least, to take up one's cross required accepting that you'd probably die because of your association with Jesus. No doubt this seems strange and a little extreme to our ears, but in a world where God's love puts evil on notice, we probably ought to expect a little backlash.

I have a wife named Beth and a daughter named Claire. If you don't love them, you don't love me. Simple enough? In the same way, if we fail to love one another, we don't love God.

But what we said earlier about the kingdom of God is also true regarding love for one another: "Love" isn't an empty container we can fill with however we already think people should treat each other. Jesus gets to define what loving one another looks like, and below are four ways he does so.

Humility and Service

Jesus once assumed the position of a household slave, bent down on his knees with a bowl of water and a towel, and with his bare hands scrubbed his disciples' grubby feet. In case anyone didn't get the point, Jesus explained: *"Now that I, your Lord and Teacher, have washed your feet, you also should wash one another's feet. I have set you an example that you should do as I have done for you.... A new command I give you: Love one another. As I have loved you, so you must love one another. By this everyone will know that you are my disciples, if you love one another"* (John 13.14-15, 34-35). With this move and these words Jesus marked out one of the most distinctive aspects of God's kingdom: humble willingness to serve in *any* way that's needed.

Another time, two of Jesus' disciples — or their mother, depending on who is telling the story! — came to him and asked to sit on his right and left hands, which means they wanted the most prestigious seats in the palace (Mark 10.35-45; also Matthew 20.20-28). In response Jesus pulled together the future leaders of his movement and said:

> *"You know that those who are regarded as rulers of the Gentiles lord it over them, and their high officials exercise authority over them. Not so with you. Instead, whoever wants to become great among you must be your servant, and whoever wants to be first must be slave of all. For even the Son of Man did not come to be served, but to serve, and to give his life as a ransom for many."*

To love one another is to serve one another. Kingdom people serve one another. As Jesus' words and actions attest, in this upside-down kingdom, serving one another's needs—whether large, mundane, or gross—defines both greatness and leadership (see also Matthew 18.1-5; Luke 22.24-30). Let me say that again. Neither money nor power nor talent nor style nor size, but rather humble and sacrificial service, identifies both greatness and leadership in the kingdom of God. As we learn in the oxymoronic story of "the good Samaritan," folks in need take precedence over our places to go, people to see, and things to do (Luke 10.25-37). No love is greater than someone laying down their agenda, their suspicions, their to-do list—indeed their very life—for their friends (John 15.12-13).

Sexual Fidelity

A second aspect of loving one another kingdom-style concerns our sex lives. Jesus never went into much detail on this issue and we don't need to spend a great deal of time on it either. His teachings regarding marriage, singleness, lust, and divorce affirm what we'd consider a fairly traditional sexual ethic (see Matthew 5.27-32; 19.1-12; Mark 10.1-12). At the baseline, marriage is the context for sex, so if you're not married Jesus doesn't want you having any. And if you are married, everyone except your spouse is off limits.

Unfortunately, this truth often feeds a very sinful self-justification for many heterosexual married folks who routinely and unrepentantly transgress Jesus' sexual teachings in other ways. Jesus goes beyond the letter of Moses' laws about adultery, for example, by taking on the fairly universal sin of lust: wanting to have what isn't yours, wanting to have what has been committed to someone else. Key here are the words *wanting to have*, for lust reduces people to mere objects for our own pleasure. People aren't objects. People are people. And people don't belong to you.

Two more points need to be mentioned. First, Jesus takes back an ancient concession Moses made regarding divorce (Matthew 19.1-12; Mark 10.1-12). Moses had taught that a man may divorce his wife for any reason so long as he gives her a certificate to make it official and thus free her to marry someone else (Deuteronomy 24.1-5). Otherwise she was stuck to fend for herself, most likely being forced into prostitution to pay the bills.

The law sought to protect the woman as much as possible. Jesus intensifies Moses' law by refusing to allow divorce except in cases of marital unfaithfulness. In other words, you can't just drop a spouse you'd rather not stay married to. Kingdom love honors one's covenants and endures to the end.

Second, in the same context Jesus also offers some interesting and rather cryptic remarks about singleness (after a hilarious comment from the disciples, by the way). Basically, he says that some people are single by birth or necessity (eunuchs), but others stay single for the sake of commitment to the kingdom of God. Whether he's talking about a lifelong commitment or a temporary one, the point is clear: Singleness is not a curse but rather an opportunity to serve God in unique ways unavailable to married people (see also 1 Corinthians 7.25-40.)

In all these ways Jesus' kingdom vision makes much of love in the form of sexual purity and covenantal faithfulness — to God himself, to our spouses, and to everyone else.

Compassion and Justice

Though Jesus turned out to be much more than a prophet, he was not less than a prophet (Matthew 13.53-58; 21.46; Luke 7.16-17; 13.33; 24.18-19). As such we'd expect Jesus to speak for the poor and needy and against those who oppress and ignore them (see, for a tiny sampling, Amos 4.1-3; 5.11-12, 21-24; Isaiah 10.1-3; Jeremiah 5.26-29; Ezekiel 16.49). Like Amos, Isaiah, Micah, and others before him, we've already seen Jesus denounce Israel's leaders in particular for exploiting the poor (Luke 11.39-42; John 2.13-17; Isaiah 3.14-15; Micah 3.9-12).

Let's build on this by taking another look at Jesus' inaugural address in Luke 4.16-21. Remember how he read Isaiah 61 all dramatic-like, saying, *"Today, this Scripture is fulfilled in your hearing"*? What we haven't yet mentioned is that two lines Jesus quotes from Isaiah 61 — *to proclaim freedom for captives* and *the year of the Lord's favor* — in all likelihood allude to Leviticus 25 and something called "the year of Jubilee." Every fiftieth year, Israel was supposed to cancel all debts and return property to its original inhabitants. Check out Leviticus 25.8-13:

"Count off seven sabbath years — seven times seven years — so that the seven sabbath years amount to a period of forty-nine

years. Then have the trumpet sounded everywhere on the tenth day of the seventh month; on the Day of Atonement sound the trumpet throughout your land. Consecrate the fiftieth year and proclaim liberty throughout the land to all its inhabitants. It shall be a jubilee for you; each of you is to return to your family property and to your own clan. The fiftieth year shall be a jubilee for you; do not sow and do not reap what grows of itself or harvest the untended vines. For it is a jubilee and is to be holy for you; eat only what is taken directly from the fields. In this Year of Jubilee everyone is to return to their own property."

We have no indication that Jesus actually tried to get Jubilee implemented as public policy. What we do find, however, is Jesus calling for Jubilee-like practices within his own movement. This may very well be the key that unlocks Jesus' instructions to a certain wealthy fellow in search of eternal life, *"Go, sell everything you have and give to the poor, and you will have treasure in heaven. Then come, follow me"* (Mark 10.21). Tragically, the man's face fell and he walked away sad, *because he had great wealth* (10.22). Perhaps not coincidentally, the word Mark uses here for "wealth" is *ktemata* which means "properties." Whether he obtained these properties honestly or crookedly may not be the issue, nor is this simply a question of his priorities. Jesus told this man to return to his fellow Israelites what originally belonged to them, because the arriving kingdom fulfilled the compassion and justice — indeed, the *love* — manifested in the practice of Jubilee. For us the point is not to follow the rule legalistically and refuse to own homes, but rather to ask how the spirit of Jubilee might creatively display itself in our own spending habits and stewardship of resources.

Unfortunately it has become impossible to talk about poverty without the conversation immediately degenerating into a political battle. One thing kingdom-people can agree on, however, is that God's kingdom operates differently than all kingdoms of the world in this area as well as others. However you think the world's kingdoms ought to operate on this issue, in Jesus' kingdom the hungry are fed, the thirsty are given something to drink, strangers are welcomed, the naked are clothed, the sick are cared for, the imprisoned are visited, lepers are touched, the lonely are talked to, the outsiders are listened to, the weary find rest, and good news is proclaimed to the poor. Here inside our doors—within God's realm—the poor and vulnerable of every kind find compassion, justice, and friendship (Matthew 25.31-46; Luke 14.12-14; 19.1-10).

Reconciliation and Forgiveness

Let me state something obvious: It is impossible for people to live together in the way Jesus prescribes and always get along. There will be fights over who gets what kind of help, disagreements about how to interpret this or that command, hurt feelings, passive-aggressive attacks, and the like. Thankfully, Jesus' kingdom doesn't leave us on our own when it comes to conflict. Jesus' instructions on this issue are fairly simple to understand, even if practicing them takes quite a bit of effort and even more love. Pulling together Jesus' teachings in Matthew 5.23-24, 7.1-5, and 18.15-17, conflict in the kingdom of God follows a simple four-step process:

First, you examine your own life and remember your own weaknesses, annoying tendencies, and sin. You inspect your heart—and perhaps invite other to inspect it as well—in search of pride or arrogance or judgmentalism. You determine which of your own faults you may be hiding by drawing attention to someone else's. To use Jesus' language, you remove the plank from your own eye so you can actually see clearly enough to help others identify their specks. And for the record, it's wise always to regard your own sins as planks and your neighbor's as specks.

Second, whether you're dealing with sin or a more general offence, you go directly to the person and talk to them about it, whether you're the one offended or you think you've offended someone else. You don't talk to everyone else about it. You don't subtly make your point through sarcasm or silent treatment. You don't endlessly ignore or avoid the difficult conversation. You initiate it. You then engage in honest two-way dialogue in an attempt to reach some sort of peaceful agreement, even if the agreement is to respectfully disagree (and at times even part ways in some capacity). During this process you may often find that the problem is not with the other person but with you, which offers a wonderful opportunity for transformation.

Third, if a one-on-one conversation doesn't resolve the issue, you seek the help of your community. You bring along a mediator — someone to facilitate genuine dialogue and to help move the conversation toward reconciliation. During this process both "sides" must remain authentically open to the truth, even if the truth isn't immediately desirable or comforting. If a single mediator doesn't work, invite more of the community to help (particularly in the case of ongoing or unrepentant sin).

Fourth, in a situation of obvious sin, where a person refuses to align themselves with the church's obedience to the ways of God's kingdom, you formally acknowledge their separation from the community. They continue to be an object of the community's love, but in a way different than if they'd chosen to remain within the family.

Reconciliation remains the goal during this entire process. Also, and perhaps most importantly, conflict presents endless opportunities to exercise Jesus' many teachings on forgiveness. (See especially Luke 17.3-4 and Matthew 18.21-35, which follows on the heels of one of the conflict passages we just unpacked; also Matthew 6.12, 14-15; Mark 11.25; Luke 6.37; 23.34; John 20.22-23.)

At every turn, practicing kingdom-style reconciliation and forgiveness manifests a gritty and atypical love. Normally we'd just sweep junk under the rug and move on. In God's kingdom, however, we value people, and therefore relationships, too much not to engage in the sometimes long, tedious, and painful process of working through conflict toward reconciliation.

All this loving of one another is beautiful and difficult, to be sure. But Jesus didn't stop here.

LOVE YOUR ENEMIES

One of the most unique features of Jesus' kingdom revolution was his expansion of the boundaries around who qualifies as an object of our love. Truth be told, expanded isn't a strong enough word to describe what Jesus did to these borders. He exploded them.

"You have heard that it was said, 'Love your neighbor and hate your enemy.' But I tell you, love your enemies and pray for those who persecute you, that you may be children of your

Father in heaven. He causes his sun to rise on the evil and the good, and sends rain on the righteous and the unrighteous. If you love those who love you, what reward will you get? Are not even the tax collectors doing that? And if you greet only your own people, what are you doing more than others? Do not even pagans do that? Be perfect, therefore, as your heavenly Father is perfect."

Whether we admit it or not, all of us have limits to who we will actively love. Certain folks find themselves outside of our exclusive circle of love, be they in-laws, neighbors, particularly slow cashiers, people of a different age, style, or race, or whomever. The presence of God's kingdom breaks those limits and obliterates our circle (Matthew 5.38-48; Luke 6.26-36). Obviously the Jews who were listening to Jesus knew he was talking about the Romans — their oppressors, the ones they hoped God would soon judge. But, to say it again, Jesus redefined these adversaries as objects of love. Kingdom people are to love *perfectly* — or in what would be a better translation, *completely, evenly, without bias or partiality* — just as God loves perfectly.

In particular, Jesus seems to go after his Jewish family and friends who are bent on revolt. Notice what he says just before the quote above in Matthew 5.38-42:

"You have heard that it was said, 'Eye for eye, and tooth for tooth.' But I tell you, do not resist an evil person. If anyone slaps you on the right cheek, turn to them the other cheek also. And if anyone wants to sue you and take your shirt, hand over your coat as well. If anyone forces you to go one mile, go with them two miles. Give to the one who asks you, and do not turn away from the one who wants to borrow from you."

The term translated "resist" refers to armed rebellion — taking up arms in fierce defense of self and sanctity. It was the kind of thing some Jews knew all too well. But Jesus calls off the type of revolution that merely repeats the sins of the oppressor and replaces it with a deeper revolution set on fire by love — not a soft or weak love, mind you, but a love that just as fiercely refuses to retaliate.

It's essential to note that Jesus doesn't ask his people to assume the role of a doormat or to "do nothing" when under attack. His practical examples make this clear. Note especially the details of Jesus' famous "turn the other cheek" teaching. He says *if someone strikes you on your **right** cheek*, which can only happen in one of two ways: a left hook (uncommon in a culture like theirs) or a backhand. The conflict Jesus envisions is one in which a superior abuses his power. The response Jesus recommends doesn't match the striker's aggression, but neither does it wilt before him. On the contrary, Jesus says to offer your other cheek — your *left* cheek, which says in effect, "I may not be able to stop you from hitting me, but I won't hate you back and you will acknowledge me as an equal, not an inferior." Given the details of Jesus' instruction, turning the other cheek draws attention to the evil being committed by the person in a position of power. Jesus doesn't eliminate the situation's danger — remember, he warned that following him might cost us everything — but he does clarify the only way to resist evil without repeating it.[4]

Jesus' brand of enemy love does many things. First and most importantly, it demonstrates the kind of radical love God revealed to the world in Jesus. Second, it witnesses to a kingdom truly not of this world (John 18.33-37). Third, looking ahead a few chapters, it witnesses to our ultimate faith in God's ability to take care of us through resurrection, so much so that we can risk losing our lives for the sake of borderless love. Fourth, it provides our aggressors a chance to see the evil of their ways and repent. In a sense this is merely Jesus' teaching on reconciliation and forgiveness repackaged for situations where one party really has it out for the other. In these cases, kingdom love possesses a shock value that potentially transforms enemies into friends. It finds creative and unique ways to overcome evil with good.

Jesus' other examples illustrate this latter point well. If someone sues you for your shirt, he says, give them your coat too. What his original hearers knew was that Jews typically wore

---

[4] Jesus suggests something like what we call silent protest, direct action, or creative conflict transformation. Think of Rosa Parks' refusal to sit at the back of the bus, for instance. She didn't retaliate or fight evil with evil, but she did offer an arguably more powerful form of resistance to hatred and injustice.

only two pieces of clothing. Translation: If you do what Jesus says, you'll be naked. In that case, not only is the mean person shamed for looking on your nakedness (see Genesis 9.18-24), he also must come to grips with the hopeless situation he's put you in. (How will you stay warm at night?) Similarly, when a Roman soldier forces you to carry his pack one mile (which they were legally allowed to do), offer to carry it two. At the very least, you'll shock them with unexpected generosity that makes no sense according to the rules of their kingdom.

JESUS OUR TEACHER

Jesus is indeed a magnificent Teacher. The Gospel writers express this truth in many creative ways, perhaps none more than Matthew. If you take a bird's eye view of Matthew' Gospel, you'll notice an alternating cycle of teaching, action, teaching, action, etc. More specifically, Matthew presents the teachings of Jesus in *five* blocks: chapters 5-7, 10, 13, 18, 23-25. In this way he semi-subtly draws attention to Jesus as a new Moses. Moses, of course, was the one through whom God originally revealed his commands, which are recorded in the first *five* books of the Bible: Genesis, Exodus, Leviticus, Numbers, and Deuteronomy. Through Moses, God gave Israel the Law to mark them out as his special people. By following God's commands she would become "a kingdom of priests and a holy nation," thus presenting an attractive and life-giving alternative way of life so that others would take note and praise God (Exodus 19.3-6; Deuteronomy 4.5-8). In Jesus, God has fully and finally completed this process, revealing to us the most excellent way — the way of radical Godlike love — so that we might faithfully fulfill our task. As Jesus told his followers in what would become Matthew 5.14-16:

> *"You are the light of the world. A town built on a hill cannot be hidden. Neither do people light a lamp and put it under a bowl. Instead they put it on its stand, and it gives light to everyone in the house. In the same way, let your light shine before others, that they may see your good deeds and glorify your Father in heaven."*

Six

WHY DID JESUS DIE?

So far we've covered quite a bit of ground in a relatively short amount of pages. The first two chapters set the stage for a thoughtful exploration of Jesus. In chapter one, we learned the story Jesus came from — the narrative of God seeking a kingdom that would honor his name by mirroring his goodness and love. When human rebellion scorched his original plan for creation, God chose one nation to be his special people. Through them he would restore the world. The many twists and turns of their story took us through the rest of chapter one and into chapter two, where we dug into the times Jesus inhabited. We examined what God's people in Jesus' day hoped for and expected from God and, by extension, from any would-be Messiah: rescue, rebuild, re-gather, and resurrect. In chapters three through five, we unfolded the mission of Jesus. He came to announce and demonstrate the arrival God's kingdom. God's centuries-long plan had reached its climax when he established his reign on earth through Jesus. We catch glimpses of God's perfect rule in Jesus' miracles, meals, teachings, and other facets of his ministry.

What's more, as indicated from the beginning, God's kingdom would be rooted and fleshed out in a community who aligned with the peculiar rule of this king. So to establish God's kingdom, Jesus sought the restoration of God's chosen people as well as their reformation unto faithfulness. Both restoration and reformation centered in Jesus himself and fidelity to his agenda. His people are redefined as all who believe in him and follow his teachings. The dark edge of Jesus' program consisted in warning those who continued to reject God's ways as revealed in Jesus. They would be released to the consequences of their refusal. And so God's wrath would fall upon Jesus' immediate listeners in the form of Roman swords and crosses.

Speaking of crosses, the time has come to turn our final corner and discuss the two aspects of Jesus' life without which we probably wouldn't know his name—his death and resurrection. In this chapter we'll examine why Jesus died, and in the next what difference his resurrection makes.

Tackling the question *Why Did Jesus Die?* is a daunting task, to say the least! So let me lay out our plan. First we'll outline the actual events surrounding Jesus' death. Then we'll begin exploring what it all means by remembering two crucial contexts: Jesus' ministry as a whole and the way Jesus himself explained his impending crucifixion. We'll spend the remainder of the chapter laying out a three-dimensional answer to the question of why Jesus died.

Before we get going, let me say a few very important things about how we'll accomplish the task of actually answering our question. Put simply, we're going to investigate how to get from Matthew 1.21 to John 3.17.

"She will give birth to a son, and you are to give him the name Jesus, because he will save his people from their sins."

For God did not send his Son into the world to condemn the world, but to save the world through him.

Here's what I mean by this. Notice how Matthew 1.21, which was spoken in a dream to Joseph so he wouldn't divorce the Virgin Mary, announces that Jesus will save *his people* from their sins. *His people* initially referred to the Jews (see Matthew 2.6)—the angel declares that Jesus will in some way save Israel from her sins.[1] When we come to John, however, we see that Jesus will save *the world*. In John "the world" basically means everyone.[2]

---

[1] We know from the end of the story that "his people" ultimately gets redefined, but at this point it retained its more exclusive ethnic sense.

[2] Actually it means *everyone in their individual and collective opposition to God*, which means, well, everyone.

We're going to find out how each of these is true, as well as how to get from one to the other. Our goal is to comprehend the first so that we better understand the second. If we pay close attention to how Jesus' death offered salvation to the specific people he ministered to, we'll be in a much better position to see how Jesus' death saves us as well.

JESUS' FINAL WEEK

Before we get to all that, let's plant our feet firmly on the ground of Jesus' final week. For the sake of clarity, we'll stick to Mark's outline with a few details from the other Gospels sprinkled in.

The week begins with Jesus staging a well-planned royal entry into Jerusalem on the back a donkey (Mark 11.1-11; also Matthew 21.4-5). Here he is greeted with some pretty fancy praise: *Hosanna! Blessed is he who comes in the name of the Lord! Blessed is the coming kingdom of our father David! Hosanna in the highest heaven!* He put the city into somewhat of a stir and then went home for the night.

The next day Jesus was hungry, so when he came upon a fig tree with no fruit, he cursed it. Then he staged his demonstration at the Temple, which we've talked about a few times — turning over tables, quoting prophecies about the Temple's demise, and so on. This gesture didn't win many friends, and some key priests and Bible teachers started looking for a reason to kill him. After this Jesus and his crew again passed the fig tree, which by this time had withered. Of course the disciples noticed, and of course Peter opened his mouth and pointed it out. Jesus responded by declaring that if you ask God anything in faith, God will answer. In typical cryptic form Jesus adds that if you were to *say to this mountain, "Go, throw yourself in the sea,"* God would grant even this request. *This mountain* probably refers to the Temple mount itself. At any rate, the point of the whole fig tree fiasco wasn't just Jesus blowing a fuse. In one of his signature literary moves, Mark "sandwiches" the fig tree episode on either side of the Temple incident (Mark 11.12-22). The point is that God will fulfill Jesus' words condemning the Temple just as he fulfilled Jesus' words cursing the tree.

Then Jesus gets into verbal squabbles with Jewish leaders and some other folks (Mark 11.27-12.44). We've talked about several of these and the others you can examine for yourself, but the overall picture is that Jesus is brilliant and his opponents are afraid to mess with him (12.12, 17, 34). The only people who come out unscathed are the guy who rightly identified the greatest commandment and a poor widow whose tiny gift upstaged the bombastic rich folks (12.28-34, 41-44).

Jesus follows all this by castigating Jerusalem and specifically the Temple (13.1-37). In addition to predicting its downfall within a generation, he tells his followers what to do during those dark days: Maintain your witness, stand firm, and when the disaster begins, immediately flee to the mountains! (13.9-16). He warned that these events would happen suddenly, so they must keep watch (13.28-37).

The priests and Bible teachers continue to plot Jesus' arrest and murder, though they know better than to mess with a prophet during Passover (14.1-2). If rioting broke out, their Roman benefactors would *not* be pleased! Meanwhile Jesus was reclining at the home of a leper named Simon, where a woman anointed Jesus' feet with very expensive perfume. She probably thought she was anointing him for the kingship. He said she had anointed him for burial. Both turned out to be true, as we'll see soon enough. At this point Judas had had enough, so he joined the religious leaders' plot to kill Jesus.

In celebration of the Passover festival—when Jews commemorated the exodus—Jesus ate the Passover meal with his disciples in an upper room. During this "last supper," Jesus explained his impending death, which no doubt puzzled the disciples greatly. He spoke of the meal's bread and wine in terms of his own body and blood, which he said would be broken and shed. He hinted to his disciples that this Passover wasn't like all the others, they sang a hymn, and then together they went to a place called the Mount of Olives (14.12-26).

On the way Jesus informed his disciples that they would all desert him, but he would meet them again on the other side of his death. Peter of course boldly proclaimed that even if everyone else fell away, he would remain strong. Jesus disagreed. Not wanting to be outdone, Jesus' other followers also professed their devotion (14.27-31).

When they arrived at the Mount of Olives — specifically, at a place called Gethsemane — Jesus shared with his inner circle that his *soul was overwhelmed with sorrow to the point of death.* Don't miss the intense emotion in these words. Jesus went off to pray in solitude, so stressed that Luke tells us he actually sweat drops of blood. While alone he actually asked God to accomplish his will in a way that did not involve Jesus dying on a cross. Jesus wanted out. To massively understate the case, all this was very difficult for him. Three times Jesus asked for another way and three times God said no. Through the whole process Jesus' will remained surrendered to God's. Meanwhile, Jesus' friends kept falling asleep (14.32-42).

But their rest was interrupted by their old comrade Judas, who showed up with a mob of angry folks armed with swords and clubs, led by our familiar priests and Bible teachers. Long story short, Judas betrays Jesus, Peter cuts off a guy's ear, Jesus puts it back on, the mob arrests Jesus, and everyone deserts him (14.43-52; also Luke 22.49-51; John 18.10-11).

They take Jesus to their leaders, where he is (probably illegally) questioned before both Jewish and Roman authorities (14.53-15.15). In spite of themselves, these priests and politicians acknowledge in word (if not in spirit) that Jesus is both Messiah and King. In between these two "trials," we find Peter denying Jesus three times just as Jesus predicted (the sandwich thing again). At the crowd's demand — likely some of the same people who had heaped praise on Jesus a few days earlier — the Roman governor Pilate sentences Jesus to be crucified.

Thanks to movies like *The Passion of the Christ*, most of you know that they did much more than simply kill Jesus. First they flogged him, which involved lashing his back and shoulders with a whip filled with sharp objects like small bones, animal teeth, and metal. Next they mocked him with a purple robe placed on and then ripped off his lacerated skin, shoved a crown of thorns around his head, beat him on the head with a staff, and spit on him. Only after all this did they lead him out to be crucified. Normally the Romans would force criminals to carry their crosses to the place of execution, but Jesus was too weak. So a traveler named Simon carried it for him (15.15-23).

Then they crucified him.

The sign they placed over his head ironically proclaimed him "King of the Jews." Jesus hung there between two failed revolutionaries, who heaped insults on him along with the chief priests, Bible teachers, and passersby (15.24-32). After a few hours he cried aloud the first words of Psalm 22.1, "My God, my God, why have you forsaken me?" Soon thereafter, he declared "It is finished," and with a loud cry Jesus breathed his last. At the same time the curtain sealing off the Most Holy Place in the Temple was torn in two from top to bottom, and the Roman soldier standing next to Jesus said this man must surely be the Son of God—which, for him, was a title reserved for Caesar (15.33-39).

Jesus was then buried in the tomb of a man said to be *waiting for the kingdom of God*. And as we'll discuss in the next chapter, three days later God raised him from the dead (15.42-16.20).

WHAT DOES IT ALL MEAN?

Our initial response to such a story should no doubt be a sustained period of silence.

After some time, we then rightly ask what in the world it all means. Remembering two things will set us off in the right direction and guard against dozens of unhelpful detours. First, let's remember that the Gospels present the death of Jesus not as a random add-on to the life he led, but rather as the fitting conclusion to his entire ministry. As such we do well to ask how his death relates to what we covered in the last three chapters: Jesus as initiator of God's kingdom, prophet of God's judgment on Israel's sin, and revealer of God's will.

Second, let's remember how Jesus' himself interpreted his upcoming death—that is, by celebrating a Passover meal. Take a look at the account from Mark 14.12, 22-24:

> *On the first day of the Festival of Unleavened Bread, when it was customary to sacrifice the Passover lamb, Jesus' disciples asked him, "Where do you want us to go and make preparations for you to eat the Passover?"*
>
> ...

While they were eating, Jesus took bread, and when he had given thanks, he broke it and gave it to his disciples, saying, "Take it; this is my body."

Then he took a cup, and when he had given thanks, he gave it to them, and they all drank from it.

"This is my blood of the covenant, which is poured out for many," he said to them.

This meal provides *the* cardinal clue to unlocking the meaning of Jesus' death. Jesus *himself* interpreted his death in a way that recalled the most important event in Israel's history: God liberating his people from slavery in Egypt. In addition to celebrating this past exodus event, the Passover celebration expressed deep (and sometimes dangerous) hopes for God to repeat the favor. Apparently, Jesus believed that in him God was doing just that.

What's more, the primary elements of the exodus story correspond to what we've uncovered so far about the life of Jesus. Think about it. The exodus was chiefly about God manifesting his sovereignty over Pharaoh and the gods of Egypt, demonstrated in the events surrounding God's victorious liberation of Israel from Pharaoh's grasp. The second crucial aspect of Passover is the bit from which it gets the name "passover." When God brought judgment upon the Egyptians and their gods by putting to death all the firstborn males, Israel was literally protected by lambs' blood (Exodus 12.1-13). God's judgment *passed over* — that is, spared — the homes whose doorframes were smeared with the blood of sacrificial lambs. And thirdly, God's manner of redemption became the basis for Israel's new way of life. The way in which he saved them defined their "ethic" of redemption and care for the vulnerable and oppressed (see Exodus 22.21-27; 23.12; Leviticus 19.34; Deuteronomy 15.1-15; 24.17-22; Jeremiah 22.3).

Laying the three primary meanings of Passover alongside the three fundamental aspects of Jesus' mission provides us with an initial answer to our question of why Jesus died. He died (1) as a victorious king liberating his people from her enemies, (2) as a sacrificial lamb saving his people from their sins, and (3) as a trailblazer clearing the pathway of salvation.

Exodus / Passover	Jesus' Mission	Jesus' Death
God demonstrates his sovereignty by liberating his people from oppression.	Jesus establishes God's kingdom by restoring God's faithful community.	Jesus dies as a victorious king liberating his people from her enemies.
God judges Egypt's idolatry & injustice but saves his people with lambs' blood.	Jesus warns of judgment for hypocrisy, injustice, and self-idolatry.	Jesus dies as a sacrificial lamb saving his people from their sins.
God's redemption provides the basis or model for Israel's new way of life.	Jesus' teachings and example fully and finally reveal God's will for his people.	Jesus dies as a trailblazer clearing the pathway of salvation.

Our challenge is to make two moves: (1) going from the events surrounding Jesus' death (recounted in the previous section) to the meanings listed in the third column above, and (2) making the transition from these events and meanings in the first century to their impact upon every century.

WHY DID JESUS DIE?

As a victorious king, Jesus died to liberate his people from her enemies. As a sacrificial lamb, Jesus died to save his people from their sins. As a trailblazer or pioneer, Jesus died to clear the pathway of salvation.

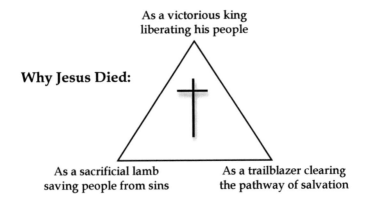

As a victorious king
liberating his people

Why Jesus Died:

As a sacrificial lamb
saving people from sins

As a trailblazer clearing
the pathway of salvation

Let's start with the second item since it's the one most of us know best: Jesus died as a sacrifice for sins.

SACRIFICE AND FORGIVENESS

The logic here is fairly simple. Egypt thought of herself as supreme and in turn abused those around her. In the exodus story God brought judgment on Egypt for her idolatry and oppression. God saved Israel from this judgment through the blood of sacrificial lambs. To escape judgment they merely had to accept the protection of the lamb in the way prescribed by God: marking their doorframes with its blood.

We are used to jumping directly to how Jesus' death saves *us* from eternal judgment, but our patience will be rewarded if we first ask how Jesus' death saved people in his time from *their* sins. As we know, Jesus warned his generation of God's coming judgment. Though called by God to be the world's true light and given wonderful laws to this end, Israel had ignored some laws and manipulated others to support their own self-justifying ways. Moreover, Jesus was the fulfillment of their laws, so they could finally become the means for God's blessing to reach the whole world. But like Egypt before her, Israel made an idol of herself, failing to shine God's light outward, keeping it instead for herself. She considered others not as people to bless, but rather as objects of hatred awaiting destruction at God's hand. In these ways and more, most of Jesus' generation failed to respond positively to his attempt to reform and re-define God's family. Therefore, God would once again accept their rejection and abandon them to the repercussions of their rebellion. In this case, the specific consequences of their delusional self-centered dreams involved Rome doing what Rome did best: stomping down rebels, at least in part by the cruel and shameful method of crucifixion.

Building on what we've learned, we can see how Jesus went before Israel and died the specific death she was heading toward—crucifixion by the Romans. According to Jesus, this particular manner of dying would itself be God's just punishment upon Israel's sins. But Jesus went ahead of Israel and took her punishment upon himself, so that those who placed their faith in him could be saved from a similar fate. He literally died in her place — as a sacrifice for her sins — in hope that she would repent, accept God's offer of life and peace, and so be saved.

In this light, think back to some of the details surrounding Jesus' death. When in Gethsemane Jesus asked God to find another way — he prayed that God would *take this cup* from him (Mark 14.36). Israel's prophets often talked about the *cup* of God's wrath, which always came in the earthly form of invading armies not unlike Rome (see Isaiah 51.17; Jeremiah 25.15-17; Lamentations 4.21-22; Ezekiel 23.28-34; Habakkuk 2.16-17). Jesus knew what was coming: He would draw upon himself the cup of God's wrath so his people might go free.[3] He would be forsaken by God so they could be reconciled. He would become the mother hen who sacrifices her body to the scorching flames of a barnyard fire so her chicks will be saved (Matthew 23.37-38). Those who mocked Jesus with the words *"He saved others but he can't save himself"* got it exactly backwards: only by refusing to save himself could he save us (Mark 15.31).

Speaking of *us*, the great news is that what happened so long ago can hardly be contained within one generation. Just as Jesus' death offered salvation to his people, his death offers salvation to you and me. We desperately need such news, for just as Israel failed to be the light of the world, we have failed in our original vocation to reflect the image of God. We too have engaged in self-justifying hypocrisy. We too fall short of God's concern for the least and lost. We too make idols of ourselves as if the universe spins on the axis of me and mine. We too have hidden God's light under a bushel of our own selfishness, pride, greed, lust, anger, and the like.

Thus we too stand under God's coming judgment. In wrath, God releases us to the fallout of our sin, and he will ultimately

---

[3] Interestingly enough, Jesus wasn't the only one to think about his death like this. For another example, check out 2 Maccabees 7.36-38: "For our brothers after enduring a brief suffering have drunk of everflowing life under God's covenant; but you, by the judgment of God, will receive just punishment for your arrogance. I, like my brothers, give up body and life for the laws of our fathers, appealing to God to show mercy soon to our nation and by afflictions and plagues to make you confess that he alone is God, and through me and my brothers to bring to an end the wrath of the Almighty which has justly fallen on our whole nation."

compensate us according to our deeds (Romans 1.18-32; 2.6). In his death, however, Jesus has already taken upon himself God's judgment for sin. More accurately, God has taken his own judgment upon himself through Jesus. We in turn accept his sacrificial gift through faith and so are saved from judgment, forgiven our sins, and reconciled to the God who loves us. (See 2 Corinthians 5.18-21; Romans 8.1-4; 1 John 4.10; 1 Peter 3.18; Hebrews 10.1-18.)

VICTORIOUS LIBERATION

In order to understand Jesus' victory, we need to back up and make note of a few things we haven't much emphasized to this point. For starters, the kingdom of God came into a world that opposed it at many turns. For God to be king always meant that human rulers — whether Pharaoh, Saul, Nebuchadnezzar, Caesar, or whomever — were put on notice that their reigns were minor, subordinate, and temporary. They were at best parodies of God's true kingship. At worst they were set on fire by evil itself.

Speaking of this latter point, have you ever noticed that during Jesus' temptations, when Satan claimed he had authority over the kingdoms of the world, Jesus didn't correct him? (Luke 4.5-8). Jesus never denied that Rome was one of God's kingdom's main opponents. Jesus simply knew that Rome was merely symptomatic of a deeper issue. That deeper problem was the devil, Satan, Evil itself.[4] Rome was a nagging cough or runny nose; Satan was the viral infection. Rome was stiffness and swelling; Satan was the broken bone. Rome was the loss of breathing and rigor mortis; Satan was death. In fact, precisely by failing to properly diagnose the true problem, Israel had become part of it (John 8.44). To their surprise, Israel too had been infected. Despite her unique calling in relation to God's alternative kingdom, she had once again become yet another boring and hell-bent kingdom of the world.

As such, Jesus knew that focusing solely on Rome would hardly solve the problem. Symptoms must be treated, but you

---

[4] John offers the same diagnosis throughout the book of Revelation. See especially chapters 13, 17-18.

won't get healthy until the underlying disease is overcome (which of course remedies the symptoms as well).

What, then, could Jesus do? What kind of strategy slices through such a gnarly mess? Generally speaking, Jesus' strategy was to crowd out the kingdom of Satan by establishing God's kingdom within its borders. If you plant a mustard seed in a garden, slowly but surely the mustard plant will grow and permeate the garden. If you add yeast to a batch of dough, eventually the dough will be thoroughly yeasted (see Matthew 13.31-33). Jesus' healings and exorcisms certainly make sense in this regard. In them we see Jesus reclaiming for God's kingdom territory that was wrongly usurped by the Evil One (Luke 11.14-22; Acts 10.36-38). What's more, we mentioned in the last chapter how Jesus' teachings create alternative communities under the Empire's nose. This, too, is part of Jesus' mustard seed revolution.

But the Bible consistently points to the *death* of Jesus as the moment when Jesus in principle defeated Satan (Colossians 2.15; Hebrews 2.14-15; Revelation 12.10-11):

> *Having disarmed the powers and principalities, he made a public spectacle of them, triumphing over them by the cross.*

> *Since the children have flesh and blood, Jesus too shared in their humanity so that by his death he might break the power of him who holds the power of death – that is, the devil – and free those who all their lives were held in slavery by their fear of death.*

> *Then I heard a loud voice in heaven say: "Now have come the salvation and the power and the kingdom of our God, and the authority of his Messiah. For the accuser of our brothers and sisters, who accuses them before our God day and night, has been hurled down. They triumphed over him by the blood of the Lamb and by the word of their testimony; they did not love their lives so much as to shrink from death.*

Just after Jesus entered Jerusalem, he said of his impending death: *"Now is the time for judgment on this world; now the prince of this world will be driven out"* (John 12.31-33; 14.30-31; 16.11).

How does *that* work?

To begin with, Jesus' sacrifice for sins shut Satan up because it removed the ground of his accusation against us (Colossians 2.14-15; Revelation 12.10-11). If our sins are taken up into Jesus and washed away, Satan has nothing left to say against us. We are free from condemnation. The Accuser—which is precisely what "satan" means—has no case. But that's just the beginning.

In the events leading up to and including his death, Jesus proves to be without doubt the oddest king history has ever seen. He strolls into Jerusalem in kingly fashion, but on a donkey. He wears a crown, but of thorns. Like a king he is anointed, but for burial. He claims to possess power superior to the Roman Emperor's, but moments later that very Emperor hands him over to be crucified. The whole story is a coronation, but the throne is a cross and the "King of the Jews" gets himself killed. How is this a victory? What kind of kingdom overcomes its rivals in such strange ways?

Consider two analogies from typical family life. The first one involves avoiding a trap. Imagine a husband and wife fighting. In this fight, the husband is in the wrong and he knows it. Not only is he in the wrong, he's made matters worse by saying some very hurtful things to his bride.[5] At this point he could admit his fault, ask for forgiveness, and so forth. But he chooses a different route. Instead, this guy tries to bait his wife into saying equally hurtful things to him. His goal here, whether he realizes it or not, is to bring his wife down to his level. It's a trap. Thankfully the wife is wise to his game, so she doesn't fall for it. If she did, she'd lose the high ground and become, as we say, no better than him.

The second analogy involves a baby and the neutralization of a secret weapon. This one *is* autobiographical. As I write this, our daughter Claire is experiencing her first legitimate cold. Her nose is running fast and full. It really is gross. But more than gross, it's sad for many reasons, one of which is that when Claire lays down to rest, she habitually inserts her thumb into her mouth and falls sound asleep. When she wakes up in the middle of the night, in goes the thumb and back she goes to sleep. This is her (or our) secret weapon against restless nights. When all else fails, the thumb always comes through. But the key to the thumb's

---

[5] Don't worry, I'm not speaking autobiographically right now!

115

success is her ability to breathe through her nose. Now that her nasal passages are so full, she can't suck on her thumb and breathe at the same time. So when she wakes up, the thumb goes in, the attempt to breathe proves frustrating, and she cries. Her secret weapon—sucking her thumb—is disarmed, immobilized, rendered impotent. (Pretty strange way to describe a baby sucking her thumb, I know, but hang with me.)

Let's apply our analogies in order. First of all, Jesus avoided the trap set by Satan that so many of Jesus' contemporaries played into: outright revolt against Rome. Even if he had successfully overthrown Rome, he would have failed to fulfill God's greater calling of shining fresh light in the world's dark places. Had Jesus fought outright, he would have played directly into Satan's hands, just as Israel had previously time and again. Jesus' kingdom would have become yet another kingdom of the world and Israel's (and the world's) bondage to Satan and sin would continue.

However, Jesus came to the cross as Israel's King and overcame evil not by fighting but by suffering and dying. Jesus was victorious because the battle he fought and the victory he sought were not primarily over Rome, but rather the deceiving power of Satan himself. For centuries this power had kept Israel in a much deeper bondage than slavery to Egypt, Rome, or anyone else—what Jesus called *slavery to sin* (John 8.34). Jesus won the only game that mattered by refusing to play the game that didn't. To overcome the kingdom of Satan and thus the kingdoms of the world, Jesus doesn't defeat them; he resists falling into the trap of becoming just like them.

Second, Jesus defeated Satan—and by extension, Rome—by immobilizing Satan's secret and greatest weapon: death. Death was their greatest weapon, their go-to move. But if your greatest weapon is fired and your opponent still isn't defeated, the battle is over and you've lost.[6] Of course this is where we bleed into the resurrection, which makes sense since neither Jesus' death nor his

---

[6] After writing this, I realized that my analogy compares my practically flawless daughter to Satan. Hopefully that doesn't put her in counseling someday. By the time she reads this, maybe she'll appreciate how helpful she was in explaining a rather difficult concept. One can hope. Not to mention the fact that I compared Jesus to a noseful of snot.

resurrection can properly be understood apart from the other. Jesus' death is not the end of his story, but rather a prelude to the resurrection. By dying and coming out the other side, Jesus displays God's supreme power over every rival — whether religious, political, or straight-up demonic. Neither Satan nor Rome nor anyone else can rival the power unleashed in Jesus' death and resurrection. He publicly establishes God's sovereignty or, in a word, kingship. God rules, and this is clear for anyone to see. And when God rules, by definition God's kingdom has arrived. Going one step further, when God's kingdom arrives, Satan's kingdom falls (Luke 10.1-20).

For Jesus' people, the upshot was no longer to view Rome as an enemy to be removed, but at worst a temptation to be resisted. Jesus did what his people hoped he would do — he overcame Rome, but he did it in a surprising way. He overcame Rome in part by revealing her true identity: not the enemy itself, but a pawn of the real enemy. He de-mystified her power claims and transformed her from an object of hatred to an object of pity, forgiveness, even love (see Luke 23.24; 6.26-36).

Rome itself is of course no longer an issue in our day, but certainly evil takes on new forms in every age and Satan continually beckons us into his games. Death and our fear of it remains Satan's ultimate weapon, and he uses it to breed suspicion, defensiveness, and backbiting at every level of human interaction. We may not typically think in these terms, but this fear plays a role in how we treat spouses and children, siblings and neighbors, employers and coworkers, strangers and enemies and friends. We lash out to protect ourselves from losing or being taken advantage of or getting hurt. But we don't need to fear these things any longer. What's the worst thing that could happen to us? Death? As undesirable as death remains, we no longer need to ward it off at any cost (Hebrews 2.14-15; Revelation 12.10-11). We are free to risk obedience to the ways of God's kingdom. Because we ultimately fear no evil, we are liberated to live and love without restraint. Love unreturned still hurts, but this pain no longer dominates us. It no longer causes us to stop loving. We are set free to love in all the difficult and potentially dangerous ways we mentioned in the last chapter, because in Christ our identity is ultimately and eternally secure. In our patient and faithful resistance to the fear-induced ways of the world's kingdoms, we too become part of God's victory over evil (Revelation 12.11; 13.10). We become walking witnesses to the victorious kingdom come.

THE WAY OF SALVATION

We're already getting into our third answer to the question of why Jesus died: as a trailblazer clearing the pathway of salvation.

Certain presentations of the gospel message leave us wondering what to do next. It truly is wonderful news that God has forgiven us and plans to keep us alive to live with him forever, but what about in the mean time? It's great to know that in theory we've been released from the grip of Satan and evil and sin, but, um, what do we do now? Building on what we just said about both forgiveness and victory, our third dimension answers these questions quite well.

Jesus reveals in his death the manner in which God overcomes evil, and in this manner he invites us to participate in his victory. To participate in this way of radical love rooted in reliance on God alone is to live liberated from the grip of sin. This is why we call it the *way of salvation*. To be saved means to be free from sin and its effects, which we can begin to experience even here and now.

Jesus called Israel to light up the world by relying completely on God and loving her enemies to the point of suffering at their hands. Jesus then walked this path himself, remaining obedient even unto death despite very real temptation to avoid this suffering. He modeled the vision of life in God's kingdom he had called others to live. He took up his cross, laid down his life for his friends, humbled himself, served others sacrificially, loved and forgave his enemies, turned the other cheek, went the second mile, saved his life by losing it, and endured persecution for the sake of righteousness. Jesus thus offered his generation salvation by inviting her to walk in obedience to these same ways. His death served as a wake-up call to rescue Israel from marching along the road of rebellion. For the most part Israel rejected his offer, so they faced the consequences (Luke 19.41-42). To his own, Jesus offered a practical walkway out from under God's wrath: when Jerusalem starts going down, head for the hills (Matthew 24.15-18). In fact, many Jesus-followers did just that around 66

AD when the war broke out, and they lived. He *saved* them in this small way, but of course this hardly tells the whole story.

In a larger sense, Jesus invited all people to become *his people*, and to walk this freshly-blazed trail of radical and sacrificial love. If faithfulness to God were a maze, Jesus walked it from start to finish and then invited us to follow in his steps. If it were a race, Jesus ran it before us and now stands at the finish line beckoning us onward (Hebrews 12.1-3). Jesus' death saves us by showing us the way out of bondage to the deceitful and destructive patterns of this world — lies we too often believe and ways of life we choose that lead only to more heartache and despair. We are literally lost without Jesus, standing in the middle of a thick forest in need of someone to clear a course back to life and civilization. Jesus blazes this trail and his Spirit enables us to walk the path of liberation from sin — the way of salvation.[7]

JESUS SAVES

Sad as it is, many folks live their entire lives agreeing with the claim that *Jesus saves* but have no idea what it actually means. Many others can explain it fairly well, but they never see the fascinating connections between the actual events of Jesus' death and our salvation. If you've ever read the Gospel stories of Jesus' death and thought, "What could this possible have to do with me?" I hope that now you're at least a little closer to answering this question. At the very least, when you peer into the passion of the Christ, whether by reading the Bible, gazing at a statue or painting, watching a movie, or singing a song, I pray that you'll remember how Jesus' death answers your deep cries for forgiveness from guilt and shame, victory over evil and empire, and guidance to lead a life of genuine liberation. In these ways and no doubt others as well, *God demonstrated his own love for us in this: while we were still sinners, Christ died for us* (Romans 5.8).

---

[7] See also 1 Peter 2.20-25; 1 John 3.16; 4.9-12. If there's any confusion, let me clarify one thing. This is never simply a matter of trying really hard to be good, and it's not about "saving ourselves," as if that were possible. As I mentioned last chapter, Paul teaches that God actively reproduces the life of Jesus in us. For example, see Galatians 2.20 and Philippians 2.12-13.

The true message and meaning of Jesus' death changes everything. It is news that demands to be passed on, a story that must be told. But this news of Jesus' death would be anything but good were it not for his resurrection.

Seven

WHAT DIFFERENCE DOES JESUS' RESURRECTION MAKE?

What sets Jesus apart from other would-be Saviors, Messiahs, and Lords? What, if anything, is unique about "Christianity" — the way of life that seeks to honor Christ's name? Many people say his teachings, but that's not quite true. Lots of folks have delved deeply into God's design for human life, even if they never put it in these terms. Others may say the church, the Bible, or Jesus' miracles, yet each of these too find counterparts elsewhere. Probably the most common answer is grace. But the only way to argue the absence of grace in all other "religions" is to caricature at least one or two of them.

There is, however, only one resurrection. Only once did a person undergo death and then come out the other side — not back to this life, mind you, but out to another kind of life altogether. Just this once a Savior, a Messiah, a Lord let evil do its worst to him and still came out on top. This is the life eternal. This is the good news of Christianity.

Without this, we have no news to tell. Without resurrection, Jesus may have been a good man, but he was also a failure. Without resurrection, the life in which we have placed our hope is at worst a cruel joke and at best nothing more than a creative dream. As Paul put it in 1 Corinthians 15.14, 17, 19: *If Christ has not been raised, our preaching is useless and so is your faith. . . . If Christ has not been raised, your faith is futile; you are still in your sins.*

. . . If only for this life we have hope in Christ, we are to be pitied more than all men.

On the other hand, with resurrection comes justification and salvation (Romans 4.25; 10.9; 1 Peter 3.21). With resurrection comes hope and healing (Acts 4.10; 1 Peter 1.3). With resurrection comes victory (1 Corinthians 15.50-57). With resurrection comes life (John 11.25-26; Romans 6.4-7).

THE GOSPEL OF JESUS' RESURRECTION

With resurrection comes the gospel. We tend to shrink the gospel of Jesus down merely to his death. It should be obvious by now that Jesus' death is, to put it mildly, fantastic news. But there's more. Think about the book of Acts, which tells the story of the early church. To be honest, much of the preaching in Acts presents Jesus' death as a prelude to the even greater moment of his resurrection.

> *"Fellow Israelites, listen to this: Jesus of Nazareth was a man accredited by God to you by miracles, wonders and signs, which God did among you through him, as you yourselves know. This man was handed over to you by God's deliberate plan and foreknowledge; and you, with the help of wicked men, put him to death by nailing him to the cross. **But God raised him from the dead**, freeing him from the agony of death, because it was impossible for death to keep its hold on him."*

> *"The God of Abraham, Isaac and Jacob, the God of our fathers, has glorified his servant Jesus. You handed him over to be killed, and you disowned him before Pilate, though he had decided to let him go. You disowned the Holy and Righteous One and asked that a murderer be released to you. You killed the author of life, **but God raised him from the dead**. We are witnesses of this."*

> *The priests and the captain of the temple guard and the Sadducees came up to Peter and John while they were speaking to the people. They were greatly disturbed because the apostles were teaching the people, proclaiming in Jesus **the***

resurrection of the dead. They seized Peter and John and, because it was evening, they put them in jail until the next day.

With great power the apostles continued to testify to **the resurrection of the Lord Jesus.** *And God's grace was so powerfully at work in them all that there were no needy persons among them.*

Peter and the other apostles replied: "We must obey God rather than human beings! The God of our ancestors **raised Jesus from the dead** *– whom you killed by hanging him on a cross. God exalted him to his own right hand as Prince and Savior that he might bring Israel to repentance and forgive their sins."*

"We tell you the good news: What God promised our ancestors he has fulfilled for us, their children, **by raising up Jesus**.... **God raised him from the dead** *so that he will never be subject to decay."*

Paul was preaching the gospel about Jesus and **the resurrection.**[1]

It's like talking to someone who's head-over-heels in love or who just won the lottery. They cannot stop talking about the resurrection of Jesus. Why?

In this final chapter we will briefly explore three answers to the question *What difference does the resurrection make?* The resurrection reveals the surprising success of Jesus' mission, the shape of the world's future, and the church's identity and mission.

SURPRISE! JESUS SUCCEEDED

By all normal reckonings Jesus' career ended in abject failure. If a basketball team loses game seven, the season is over and they're

---

[1] Acts 2.22-24; 3.13-15; 4.1-3, 33-34; 5.29-31; 13.32-34; 17.18. This isn't to denigrate Jesus' death or make it seem less important, as should be obvious from the last chapter! But it is a fact that the preaching Acts emphasizes the resurrection, as we'll soon see. What we need is to restore the balance, which we'll never do unless and until we really understand both of them.

not going home with a trophy. If a closing pitcher enters a game in the bottom of the ninth down two with the bases loaded and gives up a triple, we have a term for that: blown save. If a fighter gets knocked out, the fight is over and he has been defeated. When a Messiah goes up on a cross, his revolution goes down in flames.

Yet very soon after Jesus died—three days, to be exact—his movement not only continued but rapidly picked up steam. How was that possible? The answer, of course, is the resurrection. The resurrection reverses the judgment one would normally pass on the life of Jesus. He didn't fail; he succeeded.

Succeeded at what? Given what we've learned so far, we have a solid answer to this question. Jesus successfully ushered in the kingdom of God. God's kingdom unsurprisingly shows up all over the early church's message (Acts 1.3; 8.12; 19.8; 20.25-27; 28.23, 31).

> *After his suffering, Jesus presented himself to his apostles and gave many convincing proofs that he was alive. He appeared to them over a period of forty days and spoke about **the kingdom of God**.*

> *They believed Philip as he proclaimed the good news of **the kingdom of God** and the name of Jesus Christ, they were baptized, both men and women.*

> *Paul entered the synagogue and spoke boldly there for three months, arguing persuasively about **the kingdom of God**.*

> *"Now I know that none of you among whom I have gone about preaching **the kingdom** will ever see me again. Therefore, I declare to you today that I am innocent of the blood of any of you. For I have not hesitated to proclaim to you the whole will of God."*

> *[The Jewish leaders in Rome] arranged to meet Paul on a certain day, and came in even larger numbers to the place where he was staying. He witnessed to them from morning till evening, explaining about **the kingdom of God**, and from the Law of Moses and from the Prophets he tried to persuade them about Jesus.*

*For two whole years Paul stayed there in his own rented house and welcomed all who came to see him. He proclaimed **the kingdom of God** and taught about the Lord Jesus Christ — with all boldness and without hindrance.*

The kingdom of God is good news only if it has arrived! What's more, this "hard opening" of God's kingdom marked the onset of new creation. Think back to our timeline and remember that God's kingdom and new creation arrive hand-in-hand.

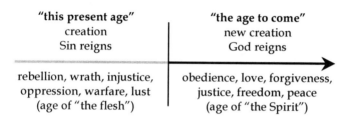

"this present age"	"the age to come"
creation	new creation
Sin reigns	God reigns
rebellion, wrath, injustice, oppression, warfare, lust (age of "the flesh")	obedience, love, forgiveness, justice, freedom, peace (age of "the Spirit")

In this light consider the following parallels between the Genesis creation account and the Gospel of John — in particular his telling of Jesus' death and resurrection:

(1) The first words of Genesis are, "In the beginning God created the heavens and the earth" (1.1). The first words of John's Gospel are, "In the beginning was the Word... Through him all things were made" (1.1, 3).

(2) On day six of the first week, God created and presented "the man" (Genesis 1.26-31). On day six of Jesus' final week, Pilate presented Jesus to the crowds with the words, "Behold, the man" (John 19.5).

(3) Also on day six, God finished his work of creation (Genesis 1.31-2.1). Also on day six, Jesus cried out from the cross, "It is finished" (John 19.30).

(4) On day seven of the first week, God rested from his work (Genesis 2.2-3). On day seven of Jesus' final week, nothing happened.

(5) After the first week was over, God made Adam a gardener and gave him a woman (Genesis 2.8-17). On the

first day of the week after Jesus died, a woman mistook Jesus for a gardener (John 20.1, 13-15).[2]

(6) God breathed into Adam's nostrils the breath of life and he became a living being (Genesis 2.7). Jesus breathed on his disciples and they received the Holy Spirit (John 20.19-22).

Do you see what this means? John tells the story of Jesus—and especially the end of Jesus' life—as a story of new creation. Because Jesus has been raised from the dead, God's kingdom has arrived; the age to come has come—*new creation is here*. And yet, confounding all expectations, this present age persists. (Old) creation continues. The kingdoms of the world haven't given up the fight. Let's adjust our timeline accordingly.

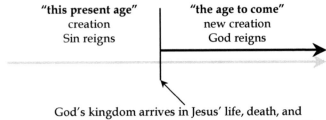

God's kingdom arrives in Jesus' life, death, and **resurrection**: evil is defeated, sin is atoned for, God's people are renewed and mobilized for mission.

Jesus fulfilled God's promises to his people, conquered death and overcame evil, rescued humanity from bondage to corruption, and reconciled us to God by establishing a new covenant in his blood—one that accomplishes the complete forgiveness of our sins. But he did so in the middle of creation's story, not at its conclusion. Thus the two ages continue to move forward at the same time.

What's more, Jesus' identity was publicly verified. He is the one many hoped he would be (see Luke 24.17-27). He is who he

---

[2] The woman, of course, is Mary Magdalene. John identifies her, but notice how he draws attention to this connection by repeatedly—and somewhat unnaturally— referring to her simply as "woman" (20.13, 15).

cryptically claimed to be. He is the Messiah, the Savior, the Lord. Let's once more read some highlights from Acts:

> "God has raised this Jesus to life, and we are all witnesses of it. Exalted to the right hand of God, he has received from the Father the promised Holy Spirit and has poured out what you now see and hear. For David did not ascend to heaven, and yet he said, 'The Lord said to my Lord: "Sit at my right hand until I make your enemies a footstool for your feet."' **Therefore let all Israel be assured of this: God has made this Jesus, whom you crucified, both Lord and Messiah."**

> Day after day, in the temple courts and from house to house, they never stopped teaching and proclaiming the good news that **Jesus is the Messiah.**

> As was his custom, Paul went into the synagogue, and on three Sabbath days he reasoned with them from the Scriptures, explaining and proving that the Messiah had to suffer and rise from the dead. **"This Jesus I am proclaiming to you is the Messiah,"** he said.

> The God of our ancestors raised Jesus from the dead – whom you killed by hanging him on a cross. God exalted him to his own right hand as **Prince and Savior** that he might bring Israel to repentance and forgive their sins.

> Some of them, however, men from Cyprus and Cyrene, went to Antioch and began to speak to Greeks also, telling them the good news about **the Lord Jesus.**

> You know the message God sent to the people of Israel, announcing the good news of peace through **Jesus Christ, who is Lord of all.**[3]

In addition to "Lord" uniquely identifying Jesus as the human incarnation of the One True God, these declarations put all other would be saviors, messiahs, and lords on notice. If "our God reigns," then other "gods" do not (see Isaiah 52.7; Revelation 4-5).

---

[3] Acts 2.32-36; 5.42; 17.2-3; 5.30-31; 11.20; 10.36; see also Matthew 28.18; Romans 1.1-4; 10.9; 2 Timothy 2.8-9

Or as Paul wrote, *For even if there are so-called gods, whether in heaven or on earth (as indeed there are many "gods" and many "lords"), yet for us there is but one God, the Father, from whom all things came and for whom we live; and there is but one Lord, Jesus Christ, through whom all things came and through whom we live* (1 Corinthians 8.5-6). We have found our Lord and God, thanks very much, so others need waste no time trying to take his place in our hearts and lives. And why do we believe in this Lord Jesus? Because God raised him from the dead.

WHAT THE FUTURE LOOKS LIKE

Additionally, in this way God has revealed the shape of our future — indeed, the shape of the world's future. *By his power God raised the Lord from the dead,* **and he will raise us also** (1 Corinthians 6.14; also 2 Corinthians 4.14). We, too, will come out the other side of death into resurrection. Our resurrection is part of God's consummation of the story of creation: The one who came will come again to root out the remains of evil and fully establish God's reign of justice and peace on earth (1 Corinthians 15.20-28; 50-57; 1 Thessalonians 4.13-18; 1 John 3.2-3; Revelation 21-22). Once more we adjust our timeline accordingly:

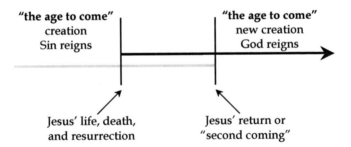

In Jesus' resurrection, God has revealed the shape of our ultimate future. On the other side of Jesus' return, what will life be like? Will we float around as bodiless spiritual beings sitting on clouds, strumming harps, and singing songs for all eternity? According to the resurrection, the answer is no. The Bible clearly teaches that our resurrection bodies will be like Jesus'

resurrection body. Which means, well, we'll have bodies—transformed bodies, to be sure, but very real bodies nonetheless.

> *But our citizenship is in heaven. And we eagerly await a Savior from there, the Lord Jesus Christ, who, by the power that enables him to bring everything under his control, will transform our lowly bodies so that they will be like his glorious body.*

> *Dear friends, now we are children of God, and what we will be has not yet been made known. But we know that when Christ appears, we shall be like him, for we shall see him as he is.*

> *But Christ has indeed been raised from the dead, the firstfruits of those who have fallen asleep.*[4]

Certainly Jesus' resurrection body was transformed in many respects, given that it had passed beyond the corruption of this world. But it was still a body. As Paul puts it later in 1 Corinthians 15.35-49, resurrection bodies are *spiritual bodies* rather than just *natural bodies*, but they are bodies nonetheless.[5] After his resurrection, Jesus ate grilled fish by the sea, walked along a dusty road to Emmaus, and was even hugged. When he talked, his real vocal chords vibrated in real ways to produce real sounds, which then came through his real mouth and made their way to his real ears as well as those of the people around him.

Jesus' body is a picture of God's plan for our bodies, and not only for our bodies but for the world at large. God will not destroy the earth and take us away to a spiritual place. On the contrary, he will refine and renew the earth so that it finally matches his original intent. Don't forget that when God made mountains, oceans, birds, and bees, he called them all *good*.

---

[4] Philippians 3.20-21; 1 John 3.2; 1 Corinthians 15.20. "Firstfruits" refers to the initial batch of a crop that tells you what the rest of the crop will look like.

[5] Some translations mistranslate Paul's words as "spiritual body" and "physical body." Literally, Paul is talking about "spiritual bodies" and "soulish bodies." They're both physical bodies, but one is animated by "soul" — the nonmaterial but corruptible stuff that keeps us alive for a while, while the other is animated by "spirit" — the nonmaterial and incorruptible stuff that keeps us alive forever. The first is the life of this age, while the second is the life of the age to come. It is the life of God himself, and this life will animate the new resurrection *bodies* God will give us.

Indeed, God will heal and renew these things too. As Paul puts it in Romans, *creation itself will be liberated from its bondage to decay and brought into the freedom and glory of the children of God* (8.21).

God will re-locate from heaven to dwell with humanity on earth, merging the two in one beautiful symphony of victory and shalom (Revelation 21-22). No more tears, no more curse, no more injustice, no more divorce, no more war, no more abuse, no more death or mourning or crying or pain (Revelation 21.4; 22.3). And in this new world we will climb and swim and play and work and dance and sing and laugh and serve — and in all these ways we will both worship and reign. We will fulfill the original task for which we were put here: to mediate God's loving reign toward one another and the entire world (Revelation 5.10).

THE FUTURE STARTS NOW

And that's not all. This future — this world of which we sing and pray and dream and speak — starts now. It doesn't look perfect, for we remain in a world of sin and sin remains in us. But we will see glimpses, previews, foretastes. We live in the time between times, the overlap of the ages, the period when God's kingdom is in very real ways both here *now* and still *not yet* here in full.

Where, we ask, should we expect to see this new world here and now? In us! In our life together, our worship and work and love, God set up a preview of new creation within the shell of the old. We are a living anticipation of what's to come, a present embodiment of God's future kingdom.

This is what Paul means when he calls the church in Philippi *a colony of heaven* (Philippians 3.20). At the time of Paul's writing, Philippi was actually a Roman colony, a fact in which many Philippians took great pride. When the Romans colonized a new territory, they would often send Roman citizens to that city in order to establish the ways of Rome. (Philippi, in fact, seems to have been a common destination for retired Roman soldiers.) The point wasn't to seek return to Rome, but rather to live the life of Rome there in Philippi, so that Roman life would pervade the area and become the norm. Similarly, Paul isn't saying to look forward to heaven; he is saying to live the life of heaven here on earth, so that this life will catch people's attention and draw them into God's kingdom. We do this knowing that one day Jesus will reappear and the life of heaven will fully and finally become the life of earth.

The Bible first speaks of resurrection in Daniel 12.2-3: *Multitudes who sleep in the dust of the earth will awake: some to everlasting life, others to shame and everlasting contempt. Those who are wise **will shine like the brightness of the heavens, and those who lead many to righteousness, like the stars for ever and ever.*** Paul makes brilliant use of this passage when dealing with the very practical — and common! — problem of church people not getting along: *Do everything without grumbling or arguing, so that you may become blameless and pure, "children of God without fault in a warped and crooked generation." Then you **will shine among them like stars in the sky as you hold firmly to the word of life*** (Philippians 2.14-16).

Don't let the mundane setting cause you to miss what Paul here affirms. We are resurrection people. We are *not mere human beings* for we are those *on whom the culmination of the ages has come.* We are *new creation.* We are, to reuse a metaphor, *firstfruits* of what the world one day will be. (See 1 Corinthians 3.3-4; 10.11; 2 Corinthians 5.17; James 1.18.)

We the church have inherited the ancient mission of God's people revealed in the story that found its culmination in Jesus. This mission — to be a kingdom of priests and a holy nation, an alternative community demonstrating a different way of life rooted in an upside-down kingdom — has become our own (compare 1 Peter 2.9 with Exodus 19.5-6).

Let me once again offer an analogy. Begin by imagining a balloon. This balloon is filled with oxygen, so when you let it go, it drops to the floor.

Now picture another balloon—a smaller balloon filled with helium. When you let this balloon go, it rises to the ceiling.

Since the balloons are filled with different substances, they act in different ways. One flies. The other falls. They play by different scientific rules. Finally, imagine our second balloon somehow inside our first balloon.

You know what would happen. The smaller balloon could no longer float endlessly upward, since it would be somewhat bound inside the larger balloon. But within this larger balloon, it will most definitely float to the top. Though within certain big balloon limitations, the small balloon still acts differently. It still plays by different rules.

The larger balloon is the world in its bondage to corruption. It is the kingdom of Satan and the fallen kingdoms of this world. The smaller balloon is the kingdom of God. Though the kingdom of God on earth temporarily experiences limitations because the world has not yet been fully redeemed, it nevertheless plays by different rules. We play by different rules because we are animated by a different life source: Jesus himself, or more accurately, his Spirit (Romans 8.9-13; 1 Corinthians 15.45-49; Acts 16.7).

We are, in a word, witnesses.

We testify, first of all with our lives and then with our mouths, to another world that plays by different rules. To the kingdom of God. To new creation. To salvation through Jesus. We witness by teaching one another to obey all that Jesus commanded: loving and trusting in God above all, humbly washing one another's feet, keeping our marriage vows, refusing to treat people as objects, working compassionately for justice and relief, pursuing reconciliation with forgiveness, and loving even our enemies. And we witness by telling others about this great gospel we've found — or rather, this great God who has found us. We *declare the praises of him who called us out of darkness into his wonderful light* (1 Peter 2.9). We speak into people's broken lives a message of grace, a word of forgiveness, a promise of redemption. We find fresh and creative ways to tell the story of God's victory over death and all his friends — the demons and habits and systems that bind us all. We share with others a gospel we simply cannot keep to ourselves: the good news of salvation through the life, death, and resurrection of Jesus.

Sources

Dozens of books contributed to this one, and it I couldn't hope to remember or adequately credit all of them. There are three writers that deserve pride of place, however. Dallas Willard first showed me the centrality of the kingdom of God for knowing Jesus in *The Divine Conspiracy* (San Francisco: Harper, 1998). Then Stanley Hauerwas opened up for me the theological and ethical impact of Jesus and the kingdom. Two chapters from his many writings stand out: "Jesus and the Social Embodiment of the Peaceable Kingdom," Chapter 6. *The Hauerwas Reader* (Eds. John Berkman and Michael Cartwright. Durham: Duke University, 2001). And "Jesus: The Story of the Kingdom," *A Community of Character* (Notre Dame: University of Notre Dame, 1981). In the mean time, N. T. Wright has sharpened my vision of Jesus in countless ways. I can no longer identify what I "got" from him, because much of it has simply become second nature to me. Of his many works on Jesus, the following had a significant impact on this book: *The New Testament and the People of God* (Minneapolis: Augsburg Fortress, 1992), *Jesus and the Victory of God* (Minneapolis: Augsburg Fortress, 1996), *The Challenge of Jesus* (Downers Grove: IVP, 1999), *The Meaning of Jesus* with Marcus Borg (San Francisco: Harper, 2007), *Who Was Jesus?* (Grand Rapids: Eerdmans, 1992), *The Meal Jesus Gave Us* (Louisville: Westminster John Knox, 1999), *Evil and the Justice of God* (Downers Grove: IVP, 2006), *The Resurrection of the Son of God* (Minneapolis: Augsburg Fortress, 2003), and *Surprised by Hope* (San Francisco: Harper, 2008).

I also consulted the following works at some point during the actual writing process:

Bailey, Kenneth. *Jesus Through Middle Eastern Eyes*. Downers Grove: IVP Academic, 2008.

Bartholomew, Craig and Michael Goheen. *The Drama of Scripture*. Grand Rapids: Baker Academic, 2004.

Borg, Marcus. *Conflict, Holiness, and Politics in the Teachings of Jesus*. Revised edition. Harrisburg: Trinity, 1998.

Boyd, Gregory A. "Christus Victor View," Chapter 1. *The Nature of the Atonement*. Edited by James Beilby and Paul R. Eddy. Downers Grove: IVP Academic, 2006.

Caird, G. B. *Principalities and Powers.* Oxford: Oxford University, 1956.

Camp, Lee. *Mere Discipleship.* Second edition. Grand Rapids: Brazos, 2008.

Carter, Warren. *Matthew and Empire.* Harrisburg: Trinity, 2001.

Claiborne, Shane and Chris Haw. *Jesus for President.* Grand Rapids: Zondervan, 2008.

Grenz, Stanley. *Theology for the Community of God.* Grand Rapids: Eerdmans, 2000.

Hays, Richard B. *The Moral Vision of the New Testament.* San Francisco: Harper, 1996.

Hengel, Martin. *Crucifixion.* Philadelphia: Fortress, 1977.

Horsley, Richard A. *Jesus and Empire.* Minneapolis: Augsburg Fortress, 2003.

Lohfink, Gerhard, *Jesus and Community.* Translated by John P. Galvin. Philadelphia: Fortress, 1984.

Longman, Tremper III. *How to Read Genesis.* Downers Grove: IVP, 2008.

Middleton, J. Richard. *The Liberating Image.* Grand Rapids: Brazos, 2005.

Moore, Mark E. *The Chronological Life of Christ.* One volume edition. Joplin: College Press, 2007.

Myers, Ched, et al. *"Say to this Mountain."* Maryknoll: Orbis, 1996.

Stassen, Glen. *Living the Sermon on the Mount.* San Francisco: Jossey-Bass, 2006.

Telushkin, Rabbi Joseph. *Jewish Literacy.* New York: William Morrow, 1991.

VanderKam, James C. *An Introduction to Early Judaism.* Grand Rapdis: Eerdmans, 2001.

Wright, Christopher J. H. *The Mission of God.* Downers Grove: IVP Academic, 2006.

Yoder, John Howard. *The Politics of Jesus.* Second edition. Grand Rapids: Eerdmans, 1994.

LaVergne, TN USA
30 March 2011
222220LV00004B/33/P